Michael Price

Excel
2013

In easy steps is an imprint of In Easy Steps Limited
16 Hamilton Terrace · Holly Walk · Leamington Spa
Warwickshire · United Kingdom · CV32 4LY
www.ineasysteps.com

Notice of Liability
Every effort has been made to ensure that this book contains accurate
and current information. However, In Easy Steps Limited and the
author shall not be liable for any loss or damage suffered by readers
as a result of any information contained herein.

Trademarks
Microsoft® and Windows® are registered trademarks of Microsoft
Corporation. All other trademarks are acknowledged as belonging to
their respective companies.

In Easy Steps Limited supports The Forest Stewardship Council (FSC),
the leading international forest certification organisation. All our titles
that are printed on Greenpeace approved FSC certified paper carry the
FSC logo.

MIX
Paper from
responsible sources
FSC® C020837

Printed and bound in the United Kingdom

ISBN 978-1-84078-574-6

Contents

1 Introduction

This chapter shows how the spreadsheet, the electronic counterpart of the paper ledger, has evolved in Excel, taking advantage of the features of the associated versions of Microsoft Office, and the operating systems – Windows 7 and Windows 8.

The Spreadsheet Concept

Spreadsheets, in the guise of the accountant's ledger sheet, have been in use for many, many years. They consisted of paper forms with a two-dimensional grid of rows and columns, often on extra-large paper, forming two pages of a ledger book for example (hence the term spreadsheet). They were typically used by accountants to prepare budget or financial statements. Each row would represent a different item, with each column showing the value or amount for that item over a given time period. For example, a forecast for a 30% margin and 10% growth might show:

Margin %	30				
Growth %	10				
			Profit Forecast		
	January	February	March	April	May
Cost of Goods	6,000	6,600	7,260	7,986	8,785
Sales	7,800	8,580	9,438	10,382	11,420
Profit	1,800	1,980	2,178	2,396	2,635
Total Profit	1,800	3,780	5,958	8,354	10,989

Any changes to the basic figures would mean that all the values would have to be recalculated and transcribed to another ledger sheet to show the effect, e.g. for a 20% margin and 60% growth:

Margin %	20				
Growth %	60				
			Profit Forecast		
	January	February	March	April	May
Cost of Goods	6,000	9,600	15,360	24,576	39,322
Sales	7,200	11,520	18,432	29,491	47,186
Profit	1,200	1,920	3,072	4,915	7,864
Total Profit	1,200	3,120	6,192	11,107	18,972

To make another change, to show 10% margin and 200% growth, for example, would involve a completely new set of calculations. And, each time, there would be the possibility of a calculation or transcription error creeping in.

With the advent of the personal computer, a new approach became possible. Applications were developed to simulate the operation of the financial ledger sheet, but the boxes (known as cells) that formed the rows and columns could store text, numbers, or a calculation formula based on the contents of other cells. The spreadsheet looked the same, since it was the results that were displayed, rather than the formulas themselves. However, when the contents of a cell were changed in the spreadsheet, all the cells whose values depended on that changed cell were automatically recalculated.

This new approach allowed a vast improvement in productivity for various activities, such as forecasting. In the second example shown on the previous page, you'd set up the initial spreadsheet using formulas, rather than calculating the individual cell values. Your spreadsheet might contain a set of values and formulas, for example:

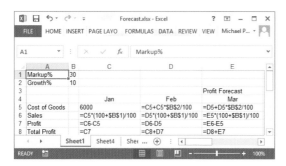

Don't forget

The = sign signals to Excel that what follows is a formula and must be calculated.

However, what will be displayed in the cells are the actual values that the formulas compute, based on the contents of other cells:

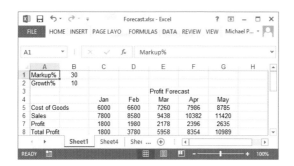

When you want to see the effect of changes, different values for margin and growth, for example, you change just those items and instantly see the effect, as the values calculated by the formulas are adjusted and redisplayed.

The capabilities of the spreadsheet applications have evolved, and the use of spreadsheets has extended far beyond the original use for financial planning and reporting. They can now handle any activity that involves arrays of values interrelated by formulas, grading examination scores, interpreting experimental data, or keeping track of assets and inventories for example. In fact, the newest spreadsheet applications seem to support just about any requirement you can imagine.

Don't forget

Sets of predefined functions were added, plus support for writing small programs, or macros, to manipulate the data. Further developments incorporated graphs, images, and audio.

Microsoft Excel

VisiCalc and Lotus 123 were MS-DOS programs, subject to its command-line interface, but Microsoft Excel was developed for Windows. It was the first spreadsheet program to allow users to control the visual aspects of the spreadsheet (fonts, character attributes, and cell appearance). It introduced intelligent cell recomputation, where only cells dependent on the cell being modified are updated (previous spreadsheet programs recomputed everything all the time, or waited for a specific Recalc command).

Later versions of Excel were shipped as part of the bundled Microsoft Office suite of applications, which included programs like Microsoft Word and Microsoft PowerPoint.

Versions of Excel for Microsoft Windows and Office include:

1987	Excel 2.0	Windows
1990	Excel 3.0	Windows
1992	Excel 4.0	Windows
1993	Excel 5.0	Windows
1995	Excel 95 (v7.0)	Office 95
1997	Excel 97 (v8.0)	Office 97
1999	Excel 2000 (v9.0)	Office 2000
2001	Excel 2002 (v10)	Office XP
2003	Excel 2003 (v11)	Office 2003
2007	Excel 2007 (v12)	Office 2007
2010	Excel 2010 (v14)	Office 2010
2013	Excel 2013 (v15)	Office 2013 / Office 365

The newer versions of Excel provide many enhancements to the user interface, and incorporate connections with Microsoft Office and other applications. The basis of the program, however, remains the same. It still consists of a large array of cells, organized into rows and columns, and containing data values or formulas with relative or absolute references to other cells. This means that many of the techniques and recommendations included in this book will be applicable to whichever version of Excel you may be using, or even if you are using a spreadsheet from another family of products, though, of course, the specifics of the instructions may need to be adjusted.

Microsoft Office 2013

Microsoft Office 2013 is the latest version of Microsoft Office, and it is available in a variety of editions, including:

- Office 2013 Home and Student
- Office 2013 Home and Business
- Office 2013 Standard
- Office 2013 Professional
- Office 2013 Professional Plus

There is also a subscription version of Microsoft Office known as Office 365, and this is also available in a number of editions:

- Office 365 Home Premium
- Office 365 University
- Office 365 Small Business
- Office 365 Professional Plus
- Office 365 Enterprise

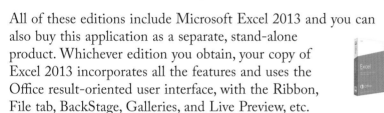

All of these editions include Microsoft Excel 2013 and you can also buy this application as a separate, stand-alone product. Whichever edition you obtain, your copy of Excel 2013 incorporates all the features and uses the Office result-oriented user interface, with the Ribbon, File tab, BackStage, Galleries, and Live Preview, etc.

Excel 2013 also uses the Microsoft Office file format, OpenXML, as the default file format. This is based on XML and uses ZIP compression, so the files will be up to 75% smaller than those in the older Microsoft Office file formats.

Other shared Office features include the Document Theme, which defines colors, fonts, and graphic effects for a spreadsheet or other Office document, and collaboration services for sharing spreadsheets and documents with other users.

Office Web Apps

Microsoft offers a free, web-based version of Office; this includes online versions of Word, Excel, PowerPoint, and OneNote. These web apps feature user interfaces similar to the full desktop products, and allow you access Office documents, including Excel spreadsheets, via your browser. They also make it easier for you to share documents with users who may not have Office 2013 on their systems. However, the Office Web Apps do not support the full feature set of the desktop products.

Excel 2013 is available for purchase as a stand-alone product or as part of an Office 2013 edition, or for annual subscription as part of an Office 365 edition.

Don't forget

The Office Web Apps work in conjunction with your SkyDrive, online storage associated with your Microsoft account (or your Office 365 account, if you have a subscription).

System Requirements

To install and run Excel 2013, your computer should match or better the minimum hardware and operating system requirements for Office 2013. If you are upgrading to Office 2013, from Office 2007 or Office 2010, the hardware should already meet the requirements, though you may need to upgrade your operating system. For an upgrade from Office 2003, you will need to check that both hardware and operating system meet the minimum specifications for Office 2013. This includes:

Operating system	Windows 7, Windows RT, Windows 8, Windows 8.1 (32-bit or 64-bit) or Windows Server 2008/R2 or 2012 (64-bit)
Processor speed	1GHz or higher (32-bit or 64-bit)
Memory	1GB (32-bit) or 2GB (64-bit)
Devices	DVD drive
Hard disk	3GB available space
Monitor	1024 x 576 resolution or higher
Internet	Broadband connection recommended for download, product activation and SkyDrive

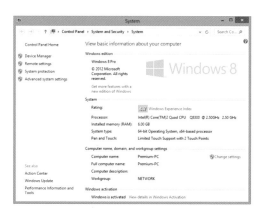

Additional Software Requirements

If you have another computer still running an older version of Office, and you need to work with Excel files that are in the Office 2013 format, you might download the Microsoft Office Compatibility Pack, from **www.microsoft.com/downloads**. This will allow older versions of Excel to read the new file format.

Don't forget

These are minimum requirements. You may need other components (e.g. a sound card and speakers to handle audio clips) for some of the features in Excel.

Hot tip

Office 2013 is available in a 32-bit version, which runs on 32-bit and 64-bit operating systems. There is a 64-bit version of Office, but Microsoft recommends using the 32-bit version except in exceptional cases, for very large spreadsheets for example.

Beware

Your computer must also meet the hardware requirements for your chosen operating system. These may exceed the minimum specifications for Office 2013, especially with advanced systems, such as Windows 8 with Multitouch function.

Excel 2013 under Windows 7

With Excel installed under Windows 7, you normally use the Start menu to begin running Excel 2013.

1 Click the Start button and move the mouse pointer over the All Programs entry

2 When the program list appears, click Microsoft Office 2013 and select Microsoft Office Excel 2013

3 Excel 2013 starts ready for you to create or edit your spreadsheets

Don't forget

Under Windows 7, you can select Start, type the program name Excel, and select the program entry, listed at the top of the Start menu.

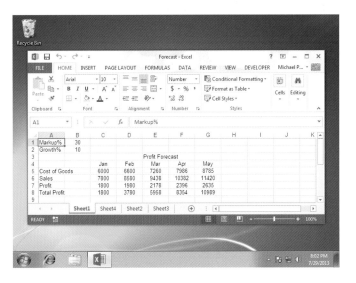

Hot tip

The Excel 2013 window frame does not exhibit the transparency effects that were displayed by previous versions running on Windows 7 PCs with Aero enabled.

4 Right-click the program icon on the taskbar and select Pin this program to taskbar, to provide a quick launch for Excel under Windows 7

Excel 2013 and Windows 8

With Excel installed under Windows 8, there's no Start menu, but you still have a number of ways to launch Excel 2013:

1 Display the Start screen and click the tile for Excel 2013

Don't forget

These options are available for Windows 8 with Office 2013 and for Windows RT with its built-in Office RT, the Home and Student edition of Office 2013.

14

2 If the Excel tile isn't on the Start screen, right-click and select All Apps, then select Excel 2013 from the Microsoft Office 2013 group

3 You may also find an icon for Excel 2013 pinned to the taskbar on the Desktop

Hot tip

Right-click the Excel 2013 entry on the Start screen or the All Apps screen and select Pin to Taskbar, if the Excel icon isn't already there.

4 Switch to the Start screen and type Excel, then select the Excel 2013 entry that the App Search function locates

Windows 8.1, the updated version of Windows 8 and Windows RT, provides the same set of options for launching Excel 2013, but there are some differences in appearance and in the ways you access some of the facilities.

Windows 8.1 offers a variety of tile sizes. For example, the Desktop tile can be Small, Medium, Wide or Large.

1 The Start screen tiles for Excel and other Office applications may be Small or Medium in size

2 You tap the Down arrow to display the All Apps screen, and the Up arrow to go back to he Start screen

3 The Taskbar displays a Start button which toggles between the Start screen and the Desktop

You can also choose to restrict Search to specific areas, for example in Settings or for Files.

4 The enhanced Search facility now searches Everywhere, not just for Apps

You can still right-click entries on the Start screen or the All Apps screen and select Pin to/Unpin from Start or Pin to/Unpin from Taskbar.

15

The Office 2013 Ribbon

The menus and toolbars used in previous versions of Excel have been replaced by the Ribbon. With this, commands are organized in logical groups, under command tabs – Home, Insert, Page Layout, Formulas, Data, Review and View tabs – arranged in the order in which tasks are normally performed. When you click any of these tabs, the corresponding commands display in the Ribbon.

The Ribbon may also include contextual command tabs, which appear when you perform a specific task. For example, if you select some data and then click Insert Column Chart in the Charts group, chart tool tabs Design, Layout, and Format are displayed.

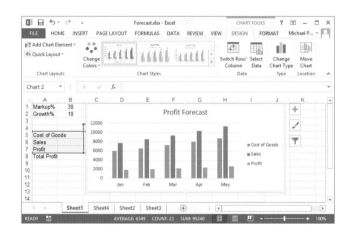

You can minimize the Ribbon, to make more room on the screen.

1 Click the Ribbon Display Options button and select Show Tabs

2 The tabs will still be displayed but the commands will be hidden

---

Hot tip

The other Office 2013 programs, such as Access, PowerPoint, Word, and Outlook, also use the Ribbon, which displays tabs appropriate to each application.

Don't forget

The File tab displays the BackStage view, which provides general document file functions, plus Share, Export and the Excel Options.

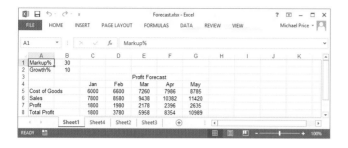

3 The Ribbon and the commands are redisplayed as a temporary overlay whenever you click a tab, or when you use the Alt key shortcuts (see page 118)

Touch/Mouse mode
To enable Touch Mode:

1 Click the down arrow on the Quick Access toolbar and select Touch mode

2 The Ribbon displays with extra spacing between buttons

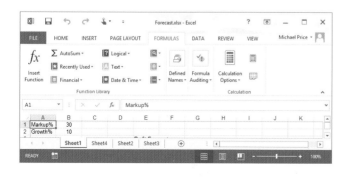

Office 2013 applications offer two interfaces, Mouse and Touch, where the latter is optimized for operation with touch-enabled devices. To add this option to the Quick Access Toolbar, click the Down arrow and select Touch/Mouse Mode.

17

Exploring Excel 2013

Explore the Ribbon tabs and command groups in Excel 2013 to find the features that you need to carry out activities on your worksheets.

If you are used to a previous version of Excel, you may not always know where to find the features you need. The following table lists some of the actions that you may want to carry out, and indicates the Ribbon tabs and groups where the associated commands for these actions these may be found in Excel 2013.

Action	Tab	Groups
Create, open, save, print, share, or export files, or change options	File	Backstage Commands – Info, New, Open, Save, Save As, Print, Share, Export, Close, Account, and Options
Format, insert, delete, edit or find data in cells, columns, and rows	Home	Number, Styles, Cells, and Editing groups
Create tables, charts, sparklines, reports, slicers, and hyperlinks	Insert	Tables, Charts, Sparklines, Filters, and Links groups
Set page margins, page breaks, print areas, or sheet options	Page Layout	Page Setup, Scale to Fit, and Sheet Options groups
Find functions, define names, or troubleshoot formulas	Formulas	Function Library, Defined Names, and Formula Auditing groups
Import or connect to data, sort and filter data, validate data, flash fill values, or perform a what-if analysis	Data	Get External Data, Connections, Sort & Filter, and Data Tools groups
Check spelling, review and revise, and protect a sheet or workbook	Review	Proofing, Comments, and Changes groups
Change workbook views, arrange windows, freeze panes, and record macros	View	Workbook Views, Window, and Macros groups

If you want to locate a particular command, you can search the list of all of the commands that are available in Excel 2013.

To display the list:

1 Click the down arrow on the Quick Access toolbar to display the Customize menu (see page 17) and select the option for More commands

(see page 17)

2 Click the box Choose commands from, and select All commands

3 Scroll the list and move the Mouse pointer over a command name, and the tool tip will indicate the tab and group where you will find that command – for example:

Color Scale — Home Tab | Styles | Color Scales (ConditionalFormattingColorScalesGallery)

Color Tone — Picture Tools | Format Tab | Adjust | Color Tone (PictureColorTemperatureGallery)

Fill — Home Tab | Editing | Fill (FillMenu)

Split Cells — Commands Not in the Ribbon | Split Cells... (SplitCells)

Excel Office Web App

Office Web Apps are touch-friendly web applications that let you create, edit and share your Excel, Word, PowerPoint and OneNote files from any browser. They can be used with your SkyDrive storage.

You need to be signed in with your Microsoft account (or your Office 365 account) to use SkyDrive and the Office Web Apps.

The functions provided in the Office Web App version of Excel are limited and you'll be offered a reduced set of tabs and commands.

To use the Excel and other Office Web Apps:

1 Open **office.microsoft.com** and select My Office

2 Sign in if needed and display links to Office Web Apps

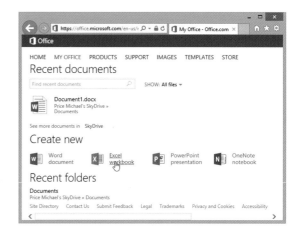

3 Select Excel workbook, provide a name (or accept the default) and click Create

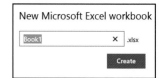

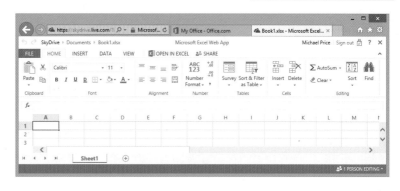

2 Begin with Excel

We start with a simple workbook, to show what's involved in entering, modifying, and formatting data, and in performing calculations. This includes ways in which Excel helps to minimize the effort. We cover printing, look at Excel Help, and discuss the various file formats associated with Excel.

The Excel Window

When you launch Excel, you usually start with the Excel window displaying a blank workbook called Book1.

Quick Access Toolbar

File tab

Office Ribbon with commands

Command tabs

Title bar with file name

Help

Minimize or Expand Ribbon

Group

Name box

Formula bar

Worksheet

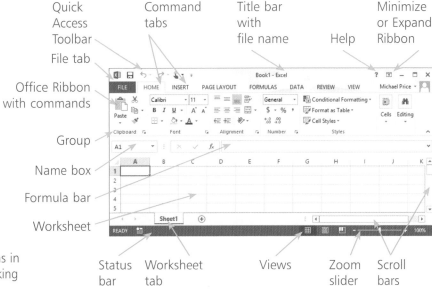

Status bar

Worksheet tab

Views

Zoom slider

Scroll bars

Each Workbook opens in its own window, making it easier to switch between workbooks when you have several open at the same time.

1   Move the mouse over a command icon in one of the groups (e.g. in Alignment, on the Home tab) to see the command description

2   Click the down-arrow next to a command (e.g. Merge & Center) to show the list of related commands

3   Click the arrow alongside the group name (for example, Alignment) to see the associated dialog box

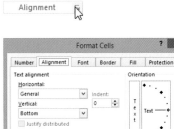

Hot tip

The Home tab contains all the commands for basic worksheet activities, in the Clipboard, Font, Alignment, Number, Styles, Cells, and Editing groups.

4   Select other tabs such as Number or Font to view other format options for cells

By default, Excel provides one array of data (called a worksheet) in the workbook. This is named Sheet1. Click the + to add Sheet2, Sheet3, etc. Each worksheet is the equivalent of a full spreadsheet and has the potential for up to 1,048,576 x 16,384 cells, arranged in rows and columns.

The rows are numbered 1, 2, 3 and onwards, up to a maximum of 1,048,576. The columns are lettered A to Z, AA to ZZ, and then AAA to XFD. This gives a maximum of 16,384 columns. The combination gives a unique reference for each cell, from A1 right up to XFD1048576.

Hot tip

One worksheet is usually all you need to create a spreadsheet, but it can sometimes be convenient to organize the data into several worksheets.

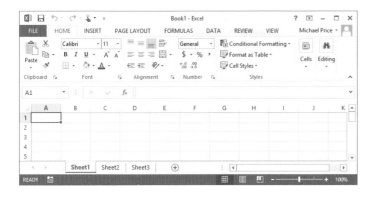

Beware

These are the theoretical limits for worksheets. For very large numbers of records, a database program may be a more suitable choice.

Only a very few of these cells will be visible at any one time, but any part of the worksheet can be displayed on the screen, which acts as a rectangular porthole onto the whole worksheet.

A1

Use the scroll bars to reposition the screen view, or type a cell reference into the name box, e.g. ZZ255.

ZZ255

See page 44 for other ways to navigate through the worksheet, using the arrow keys, scroll functions, and split views.

XFD1048576

Don't forget

The actual number of cells shown depends on your screen resolution, the cell size, and the mode of display (e.g. with the Ribbon minimized, or in full screen view).

Create a Workbook

We will start by creating a simple, personal budget workbook, to illustrate the processes involved in creating and updating your Excel spreadsheet.

1 When Excel opens, it offers a list of recent workbooks and allows you to open other workbooks, or you can select the blank workbook which is named Book1 by default, and this can be used as the starting point for your new workbook

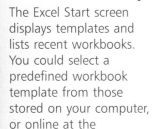

Hot tip

The Excel Start screen displays templates and lists recent workbooks. You could select a predefined workbook template from those stored on your computer, or online at the Microsoft website.

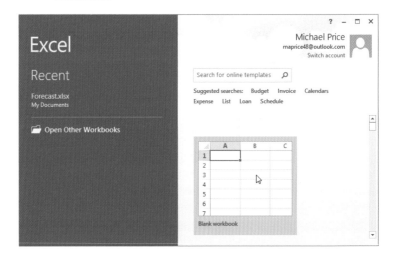

2 Type the spreadsheet title My Personal Budget in cell A1, and press the down-arrow, or the Enter key, to go to cell A2 (or just click cell A2 to select it)

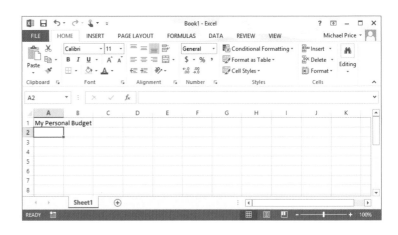

Don't forget

Text is automatically aligned to the left of the cell, numbers are aligned to the right.

Add Data to the Worksheet

1 Continue to add text to the cells in column A, pressing the down-arrow or Enter to move down after each, to create labels in cells A2 to A13:

Income
Salary
Interest/dividend
Total income
Expenses
Mortgage/rent
Utilities
Groceries
Transport
Insurance
Total expenses
Savings/shortage

If the text is already available in another document, you can copy and paste the information, to save typing.

2 Click the File tab, and select Save (or press the Ctrl + S keyboard shortcut)

Beware

Save the workbook regularly while creating or updating spreadsheets, or you run the risk of losing the work you've done, if a problem arises with the system.

3 Select a location (in your SkyDrive or on your computer, then type a file name, e.g. My Personal Budget, and click Save, to add the workbook to the selected document storage area

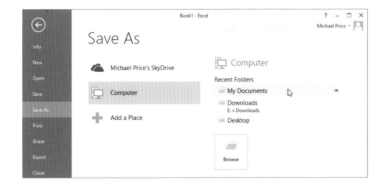

Hot tip

You can classify the workbook, with Tag words, Title, or Subject. If you create numerous workbooks, these details can help you manage and locate your information.

Build the Worksheet

We want to fill in the columns of data for each month of the year, but first, we need an extra row after the title, for the column headings. To add a row to the worksheet:

1 Select the row (click the row number) above where you want to insert another row, e.g. select row 2

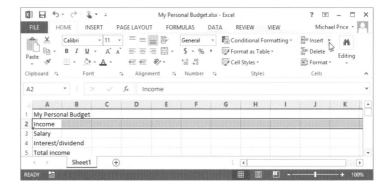

2 Click the Home tab and then, in the Cells group, click the arrow next to Insert, and click Insert Sheet Rows

3 Click cell B2 in the new row, and type January, then press Enter twice, to move to B4

4 Type 3950 in cell B4, press Enter, type 775 in cell B5, and press Enter again

5 In cell B6 type = and click B4, type + and click B5 (to get =B4+B5), then press Enter to see the total displayed in B6

6 Click cell B8, and then type the values 2250, 425, 1150, 350, and 450 (pressing down-arrow or Enter after each)

7 In cell B13, type =SUM(and then click B8, type a period, click B12, type) and press Enter, then click B13 to see the Formula bar contents

Don't forget

You can click B13 and then click the AutoSum button in the Editing group on the Home tab. This automatically sums the adjacent cells, in this case the five cells above, giving =SUM(B8:B12). See page 68 for more details of AutoSum.

Some of the labels in column A appear truncated. The full label is still recorded, but the part that overlapped column B cannot be displayed, if the adjacent cell is occupied.

To change the column width to fit the contents

1 Select the column of labels (click the letter heading)

2 On the Home tab, in the Cells group, select Format

3 Under Cell Size, select AutoFit Column Width

Don't forget

Column width is measured in characters (assuming a standard font). The default is 8.43, but you can set any value from 0 to 255.

4 Alternatively, move the mouse pointer over the column boundary, and drag to manually widen or double-click to AutoFit to contents

Hot tip

To change a group of columns, select the first, hold down Shift and select the last. For non-adjacent columns, select the first, hold down Ctrl and click other columns.

Fill Cells

We've typed January, but the rest of the monthly headings can be automatically completed, using the Fill handle.

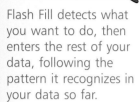

Hot tip

Flash Fill detects what you want to do, then enters the rest of your data, following the pattern it recognizes in your data so far.

Hot tip

You can also use the right-click menu to edit (cut/copy/delete) a selection of cells and to Insert copied cells at another location. Just select the cell(s) with the mouse and right-click to see the options available.

Don't forget

Formulas are adjusted to show the column change, e.g. =B4+B5 will become =C4+C5, =D4+D5, etc. See page 61 for more details on this effect, which is called relative addressing.

1. Select B2, the cell with the January heading

2. Move the mouse over the Fill handle

3. Click and drag to adjacent cells

4. Release the mouse button when you have sufficient cells

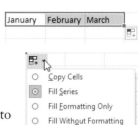

5. Change the fill options, when necessary, to copy cell contents or to fill with or without formatting

Excel understands a variety of entry types. If you start with Jan, rather than January, you'll fill adjacent cells with Feb, Mar, Apr, etc.

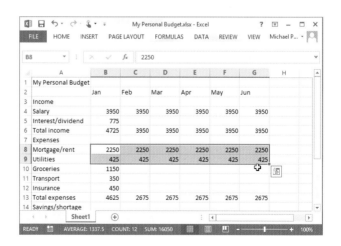

1. Select cell B4, and fill cells C4:G4 with a copy of B4. Repeat for B6 to C6:G6, and for B13 to C13:G13. Select the block of cells B8:B9, and fill cells C8:G9

Complete the Worksheet

1 Select cell H2, and type Period as the heading

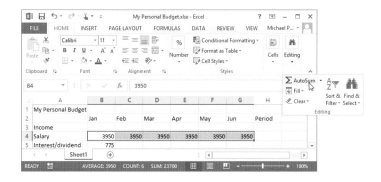

2 Select cells B4 to G4, click AutoSum in Editing, on the Home tab, and the total is entered in cell H4

3 Select cell H4, and fill cells H5 to H14, then select cell H7 and press Delete (no values to total)

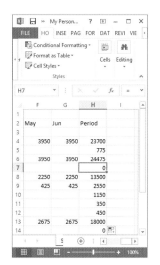

4 Select cell B14, type =B6-B13, then press Enter (type the whole formula, or select the cells to add their addresses)

5 Select cell B14, then drag and fill to copy the formula, for Total Income - Total Expenses, to the cells C14:G14

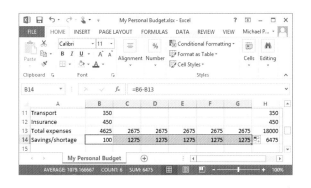

29

Don't forget

It is sometimes more efficient to fill a whole range of cells, then clear the ones that are not necessary.

Hot tip

You can right-click the tab for Sheet1 and select Rename, calling it My Personal Budget, for example.

Format the Text

Although not essential for the actual functioning, formatting the text can make it easier to handle the workbook, and make prints more readable.

There are numerous changes that you could make, but, at this stage, we will just make some changes to font size and styles, and to the text placement.

1. Click cell A3, press Ctrl, and click cells A6, A7, A13 and A14, then click the arrow next to Font Size (in the Home tab Font group) and select size 14, then click the Bold font button

2. Click column label cell B2, press Shift and click cell H2, and then select font size 14, Bold for cells B2:H2, and select Align Text Right in the Home, Alignment group

3. Select cell range A1 to H1, then, on the Home tab, select Merge and Center in the Home, Alignment group, and select font size 20, Bold for the workbook title

A	B	C	D	E	F	G	H
My Personal Budget							
	Jan	Feb	Mar	Apr	May	Jun	Period
Income							
Salary	3950	3950	3950	3950	3950	3950	23700
Interest/dividend	775						775
Total income	4725	3950	3950	3950	3950	3950	24475
Expenses							
Mortgage/rent	2250	2250	2250	2250	2250	2250	13500
Utilities	425	425	425	425	425	425	2550
Groceries	1150						1150
Transport	350						350
Insurance	450						450
Total expenses	4625	2675	2675	2675	2675	2675	18000
Savings/shortage	100	1275	1275	1275	1275	1275	6475

Number Formats

To apply a specific format to numbers in your worksheet:

1 Select the cells that you wish to reformat, and click the down-arrow in the Number Format box

2 Select More Number Formats, and then choose, for example, Number, 2 decimal places, and Red for negative numbers

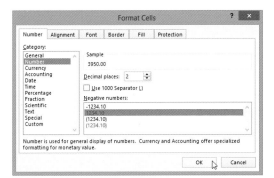

3 Click OK, to apply the format to the selection

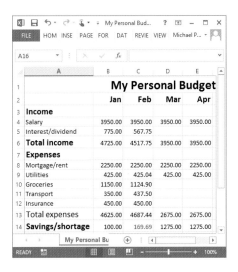

4 Change the width of the columns, if required, to display the full data (see page 27)

5 Click Save from time to time

Don't forget

The General format isn't consistent. Decimal places vary, and Excel may apply rounding, to fit numbers in if the column is too narrow.

3950	3950	3950
567.75	567.75	568
4517.75	4517.8	4518
2250	2250	2250
425.04	425.04	425
1124.9	1124.9	1125
437.5	437.5	438
450	450	450
4687.44	4687.4	4687
-169.69	-169.7	-170

Hot tip

See page 58 for details of the various types of formats available for numbers in cells.

Print the Worksheet

1 Select the worksheet you want to print (if there's more than one) and click the File tab then Print

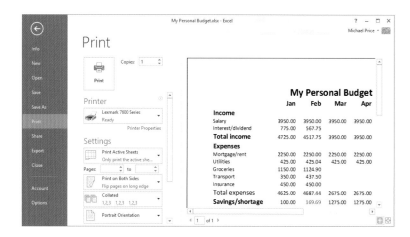

2 You'll see the print options, plus the print preview for your current worksheet

3 Check to see exactly what data will be printed, especially if there are more pages than you were expecting

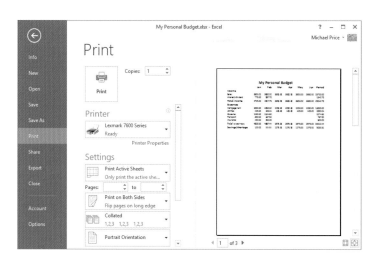

Excel will select a print area that will include all the cells that appear to have data in them (including blanks), and as a result could select a larger print area than you might have anticipated.

4 Click the Printer button to change the printer, if desired

5 Click the Print setting, to choose between the active sheet, the entire workbook, and the current selection

6 Other Print Settings allows you to choose the pages to print and to specify duplex, orientation, and paper size

7 Specify the number of copies, then click the Print button to send the document to the printer

Don't forget

If there is a print area defined, Excel will only print that part of the worksheet. If you don't want to limit the print this time, select "Ignore print areas".

For printing part of the worksheet, you can preset the print area:

1 Select the range of cells that you normally want printed

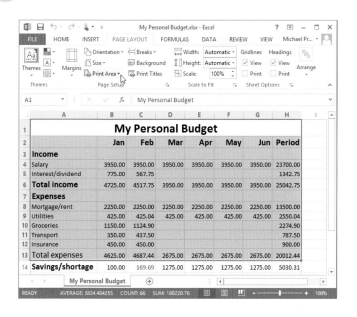

Hot tip

If you are sure that the default print settings are what you require, you can add the Quick Print button to the Quick Access toolbar (see page 119) and use this to start the print immediately.

2 Select the Page Layout tab, click the Print Area button, in the Page Setup group, and select Set Print Area

Insert, Copy and Paste

You can rearrange the contents of the worksheet, or add new data, by inserting rows or columns and copying cells. For example, to add an additional six months of information:

1 Click in column H, press Shift, and click in column M

2 Select the Home tab, then, in the Cells group, click the arrow next to Insert and choose Insert Sheet Columns

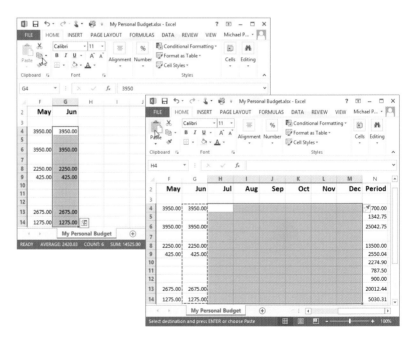

3 Select the range G4:G14, click the Copy button select the range H4:M14, and click the Paste button

Excel Help

There are two ways to display the Help facility for Excel:

1 Click the question-mark icon on the right of the Excel title bar

2 Press the F1 key

Each of these methods displays the main browser-style Help window, at the Home page for Excel, with Popular searches, Getting started and Basics and beyond, all focused on Excel.

For more specific help:

1 Type keywords into the search box, and press the Search button to list related articles and videos, listed in groups of 25 items at a time

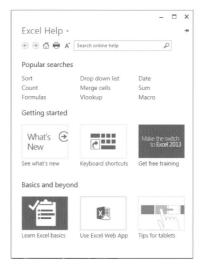

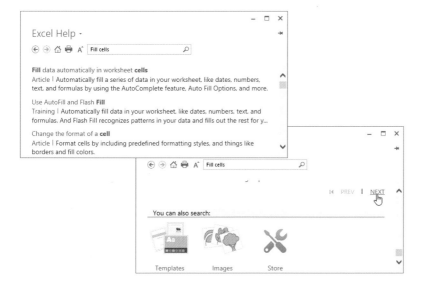

2 Scroll down and click Next to view the next group of 25

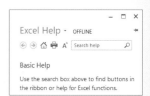

Contextual Help

You do not always need to search for help – you can get specific information on a particular command or operation.

1 Open a command tab, then move the mouse pointer over a command in one of the groups to reveal the tooltip

2 If you see the Help icon at the foot of the tooltip, click that entry or press F1 (with the tooltip still visible) to see the relevant article

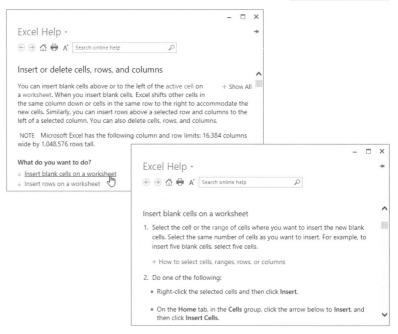

3 Click a link to a listed item to scroll to the detailed entry

Excel File Formats

When you save a workbook in Excel 2013 (see page 25), it uses the default file type .xlsx. To save your workbook in the format for previous versions of Excel:

1 Click the File tab and select Save As, then select the location e.g. My Documents

2 Click the box for Save as type, and select the Excel 97–2003 Workbook (*.xls) file type

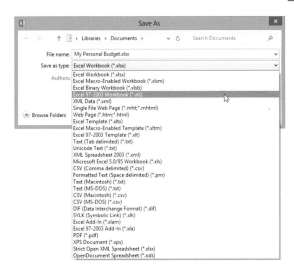

3 Change the file name, if desired, and click the Save button

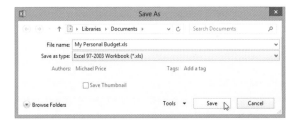

4 If you keep the same file name, you will see two files with different types, in your Documents library

Hot tip

If you open and modify a workbook created in an earlier version of Excel, it will remain as file type .xls, unless you choose to save it in the Excel 2013 file format.

Don't forget

You can save and open files in the Strict Open XML Spreadsheet (*.xlsx) file format, which allows you to read and write ISO8601 dates to resolve a leap year issue for the year 1900 (see page 59).

Hot tip

The file icons indicate the specific file type, but to see the file extensions, select the View tab in File Explorer and click File name extensions in the Show/hide group.

You can save your workbooks in a variety of other file formats, which will make it easier to share information with others, who may not have the same applications software.

1 Click the File tab, select Save As and choose the format you want to use, for example, CSV (Comma delimited)

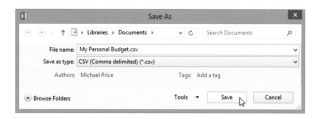

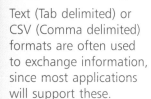
2 You may be warned of potential conflicts. For example, you should use negative signs or brackets in numbers rather than the red code, since colors are removed

3 Text and number formatting will be removed, and only the current worksheet is saved

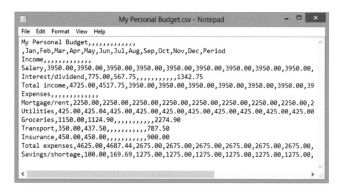

If there's more than one worksheet in your workbook, you'll need to save each one to a separate file.

3 Manage Data

This chapter introduces navigation tools, commands, and facilities, to enable you to find your way around and work with large spreadsheets. It shows how existing data can be imported into Excel, to avoid having to retype information.

Use Existing Data

To identify the file types that can be opened directly in Excel:

1 Select the File tab and click Open (or press Ctrl + O) and select the file location, e.g. My Documents

2 Click the file type box, alongside the file name box

3 Identify a file type supported by the other application (e.g. Text or CSV) and then click Cancel for the moment

4 Extract data from the other application, as that file type

For example, you might have a large number of MP3 tracks created by transferring your CD collection to the hard drive.

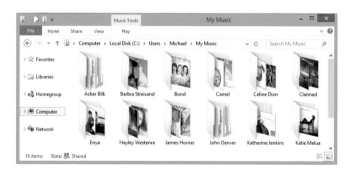

Each file stores particulars of the music it contains, including title, album, artist, composer, recording date, quality (the bit rate used for conversion), genre, etc. This information is stored in the music file in the form of MP3 tags.

Applications such as MP3 Tag Tools, can scan the MP3 files and extract the tags, allowing you to make changes or corrections to the details that are saved.

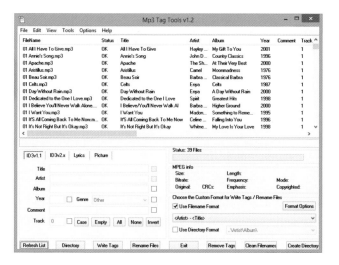

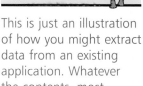
You can scan all the music files at once, and then Export the tags. This will generate a tab-delimited text file, with data fields enclosed in quotation marks and paragraph marks between the individual lines.

Hot tip

Empty data items (null values) are represented by a pair of adjacent quotation marks, set between two tab marks. Track lengths are shown as times (mm:ss).

The first line gives field names for data items, and each subsequent line relates to one MP3 file (usually one track of an album), with values for all data items in the same sequence as the field names.

Import Data

1 Select Open from the File tab, change the file type to Text, select the data file you exported, and click Open

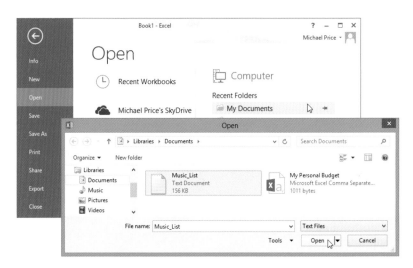

2 This launches the Text Import Wizard, which assesses your file and chooses the appropriate settings

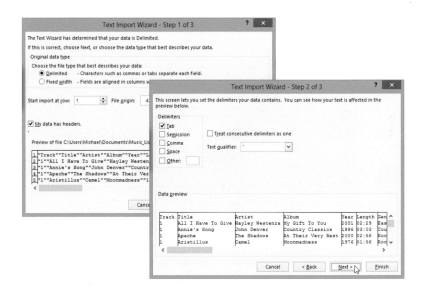

3 Adjust the delimiters and the text qualifier for your file, if any changes are needed, and preview the effect

4 Review each column, decide whether you want to skip that data item, change the format, or accept the suggestion

Don't forget

The General data format is the most flexible, it interprets numerical values as dates, leaving all other values as text.

5 Click the Finish button to load the data into your Excel worksheet, with lines as rows and data items as columns

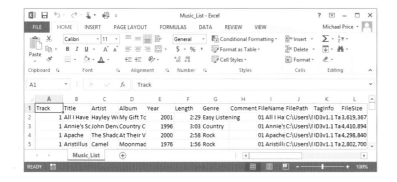

43

6 Select Save As, from the File tab, change the file type to Excel Workbook and press the Save button

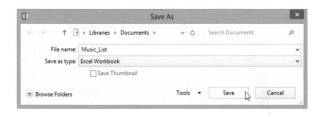

Beware

The worksheet will be saved as a text file, and will overwrite your original import file unless you save the worksheet as an Excel Workbook, or as another file type.

Navigate the Worksheet

If you've transferred information from an existing application and then find yourself with some rather large worksheets, you'll welcome the variety of ways Excel provides to move around the worksheet.

Arrow keys

1   Press an arrow key to move the point of focus (the active cell) one cell per click, in the direction of that arrow

2   Hold down the Ctrl key and press the arrow key, to move to the start or end of a range of data (an adjacent set of occupied cells)

3   To select cells while scrolling to the start or end of a range, hold down the Ctrl and Shift keys and press the arrow key

4   Press Ctrl + Shift + Arrow again to extend the selection

Scroll Lock

If you press Scroll Lock to turn on scroll locking, this changes the actions performed by the arrow keys.

1   The arrow key now moves the window view up or down one row, or sideways one column, depending which arrow key you use (the location of the active cell is not changed)

2   Press Ctrl + Arrow key to shift the view vertically, by the depth of the window, or horizontally, by the width of the window, depending on the arrow key direction that you choose

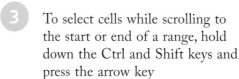

Scroll Bars

1 Click the vertical scroll arrows, to move one row up or down

2 Click above or below the scroll box, to move a window's depth up or down

3 Click the horizontal scroll arrows, to move one column to the left or right

4 Click to the left or right of the horizontal scroll box, to move a window width left or right

5 Click one of the scroll boxes, Excel displays the row number or column letter as you drag the box

Don't forget

The sizes of the scroll boxes are based on the ratios of visible data to total data, and their positions are the relative vertical and horizontal locations of the visible area within the worksheet.

Split View

You can split the window, so you can scroll separate parts of the worksheet in two or four panes, independently.

1 Select the cell where you want to apply the split then select the View tab and click Split in the Window group

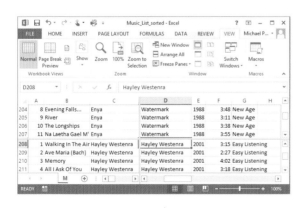

Hot tip

To reposition either the horizontal or vertical split bar, move the mouse pointer over the bar and drag using the doubled-headed arrow. To remove you just double-click the bar.

2 The worksheet has four panes with separate scroll bars

45

Scroll with Wheel Mouse

1 Rotate the wheel forward or back, to scroll a few lines at a time

2 To change the amount scrolled, open the Control Panel and select Mouse, then click the Wheel tab and change the number of lines, or select One screen at a time

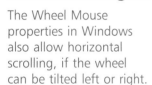
Continuous Scroll

1 Hold down the wheel button, then drag the pointer away from the origin mark, in the direction you want to scroll

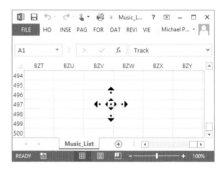

2 Release the wheel when you reach the required position

Hands-Free Scroll

1 To scroll automatically, click and release the wheel button, then move the mouse in the required direction

2 The further away from the origin mark you place the mouse pointer, the faster the scrolling

3 To slow down scrolling, move the mouse pointer back, closer to the origin mark

4 To stop automatic scrolling, click any mouse button

Keystrokes and Touch

The use of the arrow keys for navigation is covered on page 44. Here are some additional keyboard shortcuts.

End Key

With Scroll Lock off, press End, then press one of the arrow keys, to move to the edge of the data region

With Scroll Lock on, press End to move to the cell in the lower-right corner of the window

Ctrl + End moves to the last used cell (end of lowest used row)

Ctrl + Shift + End extends the selection to the last used cell

Home Key

With Scroll Lock off, press Home, to move to the beginning of the current row

With Scroll Lock on, press Home, to move to the cell in the upper-left corner of the window

Ctrl + Home moves to the beginning of the worksheet

Ctrl + Shift + Home extends the selection to the beginning

Page Down Key

Page Down moves one screen down in the worksheet

Alt + Page Down moves one screen to the right

Ctrl + Page Down moves to the next sheet in the workbook

Ctrl + Shift + Page Down selects the current and next sheet

Page Up Key

Page Up moves one screen up in the worksheet

Alt + Page Up moves one screen to the left

Ctrl + Page Up moves to the previous sheet in the workbook

Ctrl + Shift + Page Up selects the current and previous sheet

Tab Key

Tab moves one cell to the right, in the worksheet

Shift + Tab moves to the previous cell in the worksheet

Don't forget

If you have a tablet PC or a touch-enabled monitor, you can easily scroll through the worksheet by dragging the screen horizontally or vertically.

Swipe the screen to move across the worksheet by a larger amount.

You can also use touch gestures to select ranges and autofill cells.

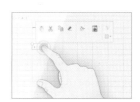

Hot tip

Display Excel Help (see page 35) and select Tips for tablets, for more information about using Touch facilities in Excel.

Tips for tablets

Sort Rows

If you are looking for particular information, and don't know exactly where it appears in the worksheet, you can use Excel commands to help locate the items.

1 Click the column that contains the information, select Sort & Filter, from the Home tab, then Editing group

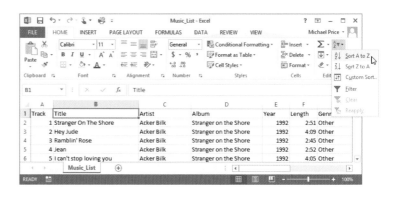

2 Choose Sort A to Z (or Sort Z to A, if the required information would be towards the end of the list)

 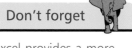
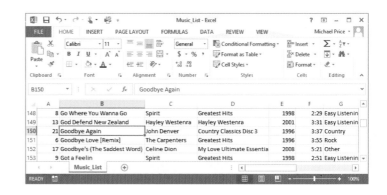

3 Scroll through the list (using the navigation techniques described on pages 44-45) to locate the relevant entries

4 Click No when you close the workbook, to keep the original sequence of entries

Find Entries

If you'd rather not change the sequence of the rows, you can use the Find command to locate appropriate entries.

1 Click the column with the information, choose Find & Select, from the Editing group on the Home tab, then click Find (or press Ctrl + F)

2 Click the Options button, if necessary (Excel remembers the last setting)

3 Specify a word or phrase, select the options, to search within the worksheet and in the Column, and then click Find Next

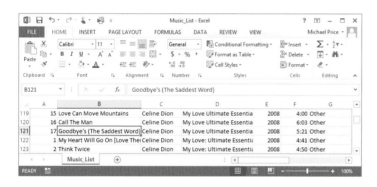

4 Repeat Find Next, to locate subsequent matching entries

5 You can click Find All to get a list of the cell addresses for matching entries

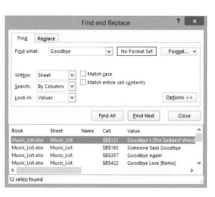

Don't forget

Select all the cells in the column; the search will be restricted to that part of the worksheet.

Hot tip

You can include case in the check, and you can require a full match with the entire cell contents.

49

Filter Information

The Filter part of the Sort & Filter command can be very helpful in assessing the information you have imported, because it allows you to concentrate on particular sections of the data.

1 Select all the data (for example, click in the data region, press Ctrl + End, then press Shift + Ctrl + Home)

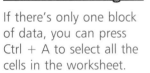
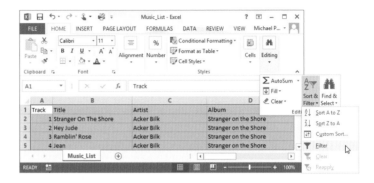

2 Select Sort & Filter from the Home tab, Editing group, and then click the Filter command

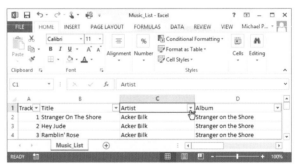

3 Click the arrow box in the column heading, to display unique values

4 Clear the boxes for unwanted values, to leave those you want to view, e.g. guest artists

5 Click OK to display the entries

6 Make the changes that are required (e.g. copy guest artists to the Comments field, leaving just the main artist)

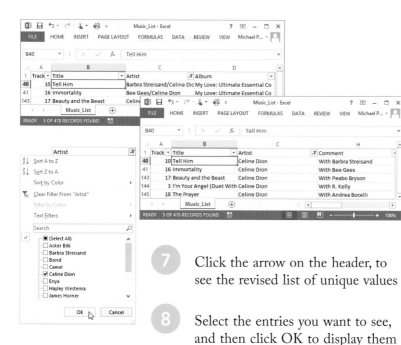

7 Click the arrow on the header, to see the revised list of unique values

8 Select the entries you want to see, and then click OK to display them

51

You can filter for blank entries, to identify cells with missing data.

1 Click the arrow for Track, click (Select All) to clear the box, then select (Blanks) and 32, then click OK

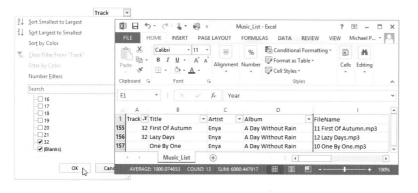

2 You can then correct the missing entries, in this case, by copying the track numbers from the FileName column

Remove Duplicate Entries

A duplicate entry is where all values in the row are an exact match for all the values in another row.

To find and remove duplicate values:

1 Select the range of cells

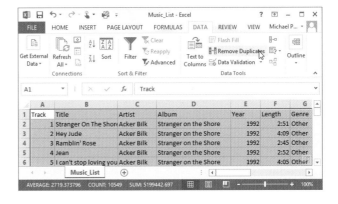

2 Select the Data tab, then, from the Data Tools group, click Remove Duplicates

3 Click Select All, to ensure all columns are checked

4 Clear the box for "My data has headers", if you suspect these may be repeated

5 Click OK, to detect and delete the duplicates

A message is displayed, indicating how many duplicate values were removed and how many unique values remain

6 Click OK

There's no Undo for this operation – it's permanent.

Hot tip

Sorting (see page 48) may help you spot repeated entries, caused, for example, when some data gets imported twice, but Excel offers a more systematic method.

Beware

Duplicate values are based on the displayed value, not on the stored value, so differences in format will make the entry appear unique.

Don't forget

If you want to keep the original worksheet with the duplicates, save the revised version under a new name.

Check Spelling

A spelling check is sometimes a useful way to assess the contents of some sections of your worksheet.

1 Select the relevant parts: for example, click one column, press and hold Ctrl, then click more columns in turn

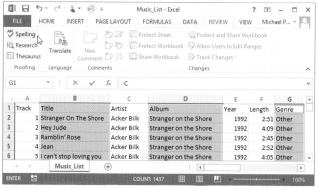

Don't forget

Select columns of data that contain text values that need spell-checking.

2 Select the Review tab, then click the Spelling command in the Proofing group (or press F7)

3 Click Change All, if the word being corrected is likely to appear more than once

Hot tip

You can add foreign language dictionaries if they are required to spell check text in your worksheets.

4 Click Ignore All, if there are spelling warnings for valid terms or foreign words

5 Click OK when the check is completed

Freeze Headers and Labels

When you navigate a worksheet, column headings and row labels will move off screen, making it more difficult to identify the data elements. To keep these visible, start by clicking on the worksheet.

1 Click the cell below the headings and to the right of the labels (e.g. with one row and one column, choose cell B2)

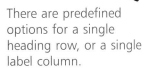

There are predefined options for a single heading row, or a single label column.

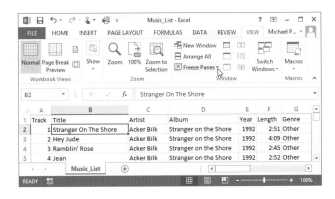

2 Select the View tab and click the Freeze Panes command, from the Window group

Don't forget

You can now scroll down and the headings stay visible. Similarly, if you scroll across, the row labels now stay visible.

3 Choose the appropriate option from the list

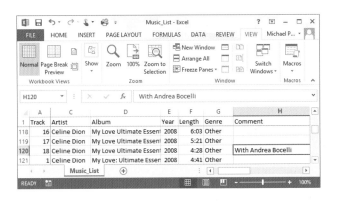

Beware

You cannot Freeze rows and columns when you Share your workbooks for collaborative changes.

4 The first entry for the Freeze Panes command changes to the undo option, Unfreeze Panes

Hide Columns or Rows

To make it easier to view particular portions of the worksheet, you can tell Excel not to display certain columns or rows

1 Select the columns or rows that you want to hide. For example, to select non-adjacent columns, select the first column, hold down Ctrl, then select subsequent columns

2 Select the Home tab, then click the Format command from the Cells group

3 Select Hide & Unhide, then click Hide Columns or Hide Rows, as required

To redisplay the hidden columns or rows:

1 Select the columns either side of hidden columns, or select the rows above and below hidden rows

2 Open the Hide & Unhide menu and select Unhide Columns or Unhide Rows

Hot tip

You cannot cancel the selection of a cell, or range of cells in a non-adjacent selection, without canceling the entire selection.

Don't forget

A column or row also becomes hidden if you change its column width or row height to zero. The Unhide command will reveal columns and rows hidden in this way.

Hot tip

You can also right-click a selected group of rows or columns, and then click Hide or Unhide from the menu that appears.

Protect a Worksheet

Don't forget

Once you've set up your worksheet the way you want, you can lock it, to protect it from being accidentally changed.

There's a greater need to protect Workbooks in Excel 2013 where you use storage on SkyDrives that are accessible to other users.

1 Select any column (e.g. Comments) that you might want to update

2 On the Home tab, select Format from the Cells group, then click Format cells

3 Select the Protection tab, then clear the Locked box, and the Lock Text box also, if this is displayed

4 To protect the remaining part of the worksheet, select the Review tab and click Protect Sheet in the Changes group

5 Ensure that all users are allowed to select locked and unlocked cells, then click OK

6 You can edit cells in the chosen columns, but you get an error message if you edit other cells

Hot tip

When you protect the sheet, the command changes to Unprotect Sheet, to allow you to reverse the process.

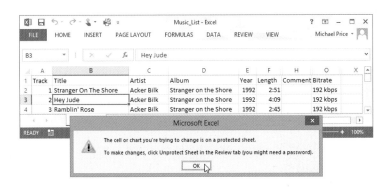

4 Formulas and Functions

Various formats for numbers are explained, and options for referencing cell locations are reviewed. These provide the basis for an introduction to functions and formulas, beginning with operators and calculation sequence, including formula errors and cell comments.

Number Formats

The cells in the worksheet contain values, in the form of numbers or text characters. The associated cell formats control how the contents are displayed.

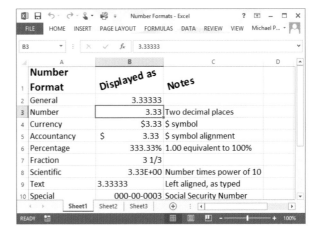

Cells B2 to B10 all contain the same value (3.33333) but each cell has a different format, which changes the way the number appears on the worksheet. To set the number format:

1 Select the cell or cells, then click the Home tab, select Format from the Cells group, and choose Format Cells from Protection

2 Select the Number tab and choose the category, to see how the contents would appear, and to select attributes, such as decimal places and the appearance of negative numbers

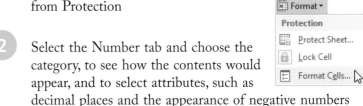

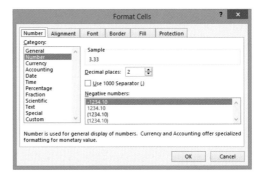

Date and Time are also number formats, but, in this case, the number is taken as the days since a base point in time.

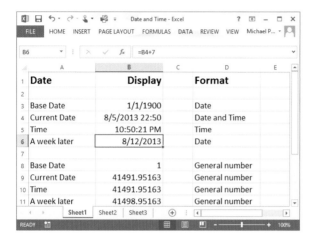

Don't forget

Because dates and times are stored as numbers, you can use them in formulas and calculations.

Cells B3 to B6 are formatted as dates or times. The same numbers are shown in cells B8 to B11, formatted as General. This shows that day 1 is January 1st 1900, day 41491 is August 5th 2013 while day 41498 is a week later. Decimals indicate part days.

To set or change the date or time format:

1   Open Format Cells, select the Number tab, and click Date or Time, to see the list of format options

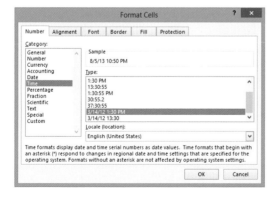

When dates are based on 1/1/1900, day 60 is incorrectly treated as February 29th 1900. In Excel 2013 this can be resolved using the Strict Open XML file format (see page 37).

59

Don't forget

Some of the formats depend on the specific country and locations defined in the Windows regional options, found in the Control Panel.

2   Choose a format option and click OK, or click Custom to see other time and date formatting options

Text Formats

Excel recognizes cells containing text, such as header and label cells, and gives them the General format, with default text format settings (left-aligned, and using the standard font). You can view or change the format for such cells:

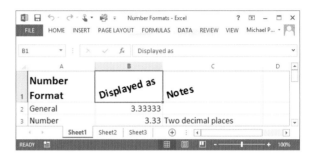

1 Select the cell or range of cells, open Format Cells, select the Font tab to review the font, font style, size, and color

2 Select the Alignment tab and change the text controls, alignment, or orientation settings

Relative References

A cell could contain a formula, rather than an actual value. Excel performs the calculation the formula represents, and displays the result as the value for that cell. For example:

In this worksheet, cell D3 shows the amount spent on DVDs (price times quantity), calculated as =B3*C3.

The formulas for D4 and D5 are created by copying and pasting D3. The cell references in the formula are relative to the position of the cell containing them, and are automatically updated for the new location.

A cell reference in this form is known as a relative reference, and this is the normal type of reference used in worksheets.

The results of formulas can be used in other formulas, so the total in cell D6 is calculated as =D3+D4+D5.

The sales tax in cell D7 is calculated as =D6*B7. Note that B7 is displayed as a value of 7.5%, the cell format being Percentage. The actual value stored in the cell is 0.075.

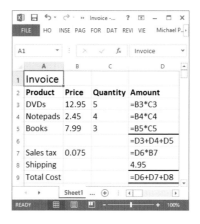

Hot tip

The cells hold formulas as stored values, but it is the results that normally get displayed. To switch between results and formulas, press Ctrl+` (the grave accent key), or select the Formulas tab and click Show Formulas.

61

The worksheet could have used a constant value instead, such as =D5*7.5/100 or =D5*7.5%. However, having the value stored in a cell makes it easier to adapt the worksheet when rates change. It also helps when the value is used more than once.

The shipping cost in cell D8 is a stored constant.

The final calculation in the worksheet is the total cost in cell D9, which is calculated as =D6+D7+D8.

Don't forget

The value B7 is a relative cell reference, like the others, but this may not be the best option. See page 62 for the alternative, the absolute cell reference.

Absolute References

Assume that calculation of the sales tax per line item is required. The value in cell E3 for the DVDs product would be =D3*B7.

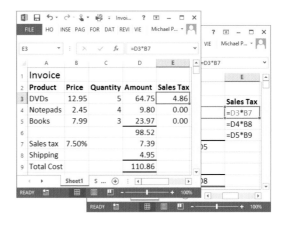

You might be tempted to copy this formula down into cells E4 and E5, but, as you see here, the results would be incorrect, giving zero values, because the relative reference B7 would be incremented to B8 and then B9, both of which are empty cells. The answer is to fix the reference to B7, so that it doesn't change when the formula is copied. To indicate this, you edit the formula, to place a $ symbol in front of the row and column addresses.

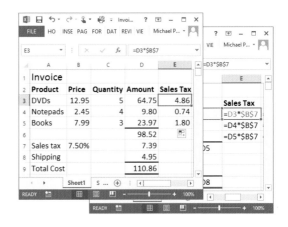

Copy this formula down into cells E4 and E5, the reference $B$7 doesn't change, so the results are correct. This form of cell reference is known as an absolute reference. A cell reference with only part of the address fixed, such as $D3 or D$3, would be known as a **mixed reference**.

Name References

Names provide a different way of referring to cells in formulas. To create a name for a cell or cell range:

1 Select the cell, or the group of cells, you want to name

2 Click the Name box, on the left of the Formula bar

3 Type the name that you'll be using to refer to the selection, then press Enter

4 Click the Formulas tab and select the Name Manager, in the Defined Names group, to view names in the workbook

Names create absolute references to cells or ranges in the current worksheet. They can be used in formulas, and, when these are copied, the references will not be incremented.

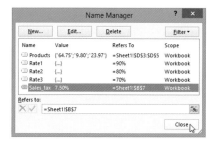

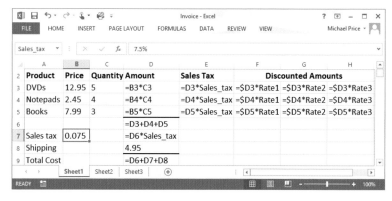

You cannot use certain names, such as R1, R2, R3, since these are actual cell references. You must specify non-ambiguous names, such as Rate1, Rate2, Rate3.

> ### Don't forget
>
>
> Names must start with a letter, underscore, or backslash. They can contain letters, numbers, periods, and underscores, but not spaces, and case is ignored. Their maximum length is 255 characters.

> ### Don't forget
>
> Names can be defined for a cell, for a range or group of cells, or for constants and functions.

Operators

The formulas shown so far have used several operators (+, *, %), but there are many other operators you might use, in a number of categories, including the following:

Category	Meaning	Examples
Arithmetic		
+ (plus sign)	Addition	A7+B5
- (minus sign)	Subtraction Negation	C6-20 -C3
* (asterisk)	Multiplication	C5*C6
/ (forward slash)	Division	C6/D3
% (percent sign)	Percent	20%
^ (caret)	Exponentiation or Power	D3^2
Comparison		
= (equal)	Equal to	A1=B1
> (greater than)	Greater than	A1>B1
< (less than)	Less than	A1<B1
>= (greater than with equal)	Greater than or equal	A1>=B1
<= (less than with equal)	Less than or equal	A1<=B1
<> (not equal)	Not equal	A1<>B1
Text		
& (ampersand)	Connect/join	"ABCDE"&"FGHI"
Reference		
: (colon)	Range	B5:B15
, (comma)	Union	SUM(B5:B15,D5:D15)
(space)	Intersection	B2:D6 C4:F8

Calculation Sequence

The order in which a calculation is performed may affect the result. As an example, the calculation 6+4*2 could be interpreted in two different ways. If the addition is performed first, this would give 10*2, which equals 20. However, if the multiplication is performed first, the calculation becomes 6+8, which equals 14.

To avoid any ambiguity in calculations, Excel evaluates formulas by applying the operators in a specific order. This is known as **operator precedence**. The sequence is as follows:

1	: ▪ ,	Colon Space Comma
2	-	Negation
3	%	Percentage
4	^	Exponential
5	* /	Multiplication Division
6	+ -	Addition Subtraction
7	&	Concatenation
8	= < > <= >= <>	Comparison

When the formula has several operators with the same precedence, multiplication and division for example, Excel evaluates the operators from left to right.

These are some example formulas that illustrate the effect of operator precedence on the calculation result:

You use parentheses to change the order of evaluation, since the expressions within parentheses are evaluated first. If there are parentheses within parentheses, Excel evaluates the expression in the innermost pair of parentheses first, then works outwards.

Functions

Functions are predefined formulas that perform calculations based on specific values, called arguments, provided in the required sequence. The function begins with the function name, followed by an opening parenthesis, the arguments for the function separated by commas, and a closing parenthesis. They are used for many types of calculation, ranging from simple to highly complex.

If you are unsure which function is appropriate for the task, Excel will help you search for the most appropriate. To select a function in the Invoice worksheet:

Hot tip

Arguments can be numbers, text, cell references, or logical values (i.e. True or False).

Don't forget

You'll find several new functions in Excel 2013 in the various categories offered (see page 88).

1   Click the cell where you want to use a function as the formula, the total amount cell D6, for example

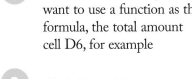

	A	B	C	D
2	Product	Price	Quantity	Amount
3	DVDs	12.95	5	64.75
4	Notepads	2.45	4	9.80
5	Books	7.99	3	23.97
6				

2   Click Insert Function, on the Formula bar

3   Enter the phrase Add numbers in the Search for a function box, and click Go to list related functions

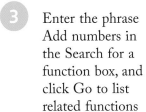

Insert Function

Search for a function:

add numbers   Go

Or select a category: Recommended

Select a function:

IMSUM
SUM
SUMIF
TEXT
DCOUNT

SUM(number1,number2,...)
Adds all the numbers in a range of cells.

Help on this function   OK   Cancel

4   Select the most appropriate function, in this case SUM, and click OK

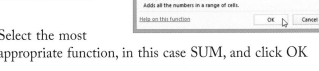

Function Arguments

SUM

Number1   D3:D5   = {64.75;9.8;23.97}
Number2   = number

Adds all the numbers in a range of cells.   = 98.52

Number1: number1,number2,... are 1 to 255 numbers to sum. Logical values and text are ignored in cells, included if typed as arguments.

Formula result = 98.52
Help on this function   OK   Cancel

Hot tip

To select or change the arguments, click the Collapse Dialog button, select the cells on the worksheet, then press the Expand Dialog button.

5   Review the arguments suggested, in this case range D3:D5, see the answer this gives, adjust if needed then click OK to Insert Function

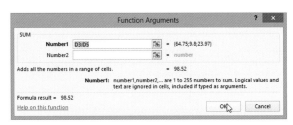

=SUM(D3:D5)

D
Amount
64.75
9.80
23.97
98.52

Autocomplete

Even when you know the function needed, Excel will help you set it up, to help avoid possible syntax and typing errors.

1 Click the worksheet cell, and begin typing the function, for example, click the total cost cell D9 and type =s

2 Excel lists functions that match so far, so you can select a function and see its description, scroll down to see more names, or continue typing, for example =su, to narrow the list

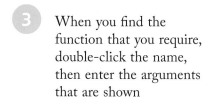

3 When you find the function that you require, double-click the name, then enter the arguments that are shown

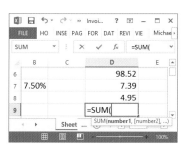

4 For example, click D6, press period, and click D8

5 Type the closing parenthesis, and then press Enter

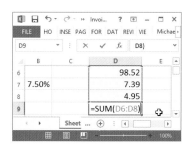

6 The formula with the function is stored in the cell, and the result of the operation will be displayed

As always, you should save the spreadsheet from time to time, to preserve your changes.

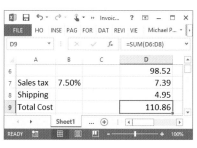

Hot tip

Click on the function name in the prompt, to display help for that function.

Don't forget

Type the range name, if you have already defined the required cells (see page 63).

67

AutoSum

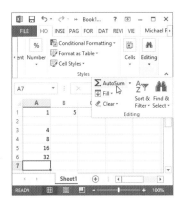

1. Select the cell below a column of numbers

Hot tip

All the cells up or across, to the first non-numeric or empty cell, are included in the total.

2. To total the numbers, click AutoSum, in the Editing group on the Home tab

3. Press Enter, or click on the tick in the Formula bar, to add the function

Hot tip

In either case, you can click the arrow next to AutoSum, and select from the list of functions offered to apply a different function to the range of values.

4. Similarly, select the cell to the right of a row of numbers and click AutoSum to total them

When the selected cell could be associated with a row or a column, AutoSum will usually favor the column. However, you can adjust the direction or extent of the range in the formula before you apply it to the worksheet.

The AutoSum function is also provided in the Function Library group, on the Formulas tab, along with Insert Function, Recently Used, and various sets of functions such as Financial and Logical.

Formula Errors

Excel helps you to avoid some of the more common errors when you are entering a formula.

1 When you type a name, Excel outlines the associated cell or range, so you can confirm that it is the correct selection

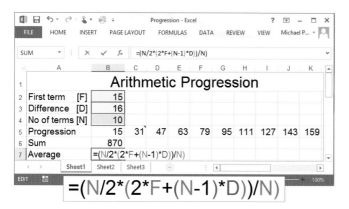

2 With nested functions, Excel colors the parentheses, to help you ensure that they are in matching open/close pairs

3 If you do make an error, such as the extra parenthesis shown above, it is often detected and corrected

4 If the result overflows the available space, Excel displays hash signs

5 There's a similar display for other errors, but, in addition, a green flash shows in the top left-hand corner of the cell

6 Select the cell, then click the information icon and the Help entry, for more details

Hot tip

In this example, F, D, and N are defined names.

Hot tip

This totals and averages the terms in a number series, with formulas that have several levels of parentheses. Here, the final parenthesis needs to be deleted, as Excel will detect.

Don't forget

Other common errors displayed this way include #REF! (invalid reference) and #NAME? (name not recognized).

#REF!

#NAME?

Add Comments

You can add notes to a cell, perhaps to explain the way in which a particular formula operates.

1 Click the cell where the comment is meant to appear

2 Select the Review tab, and click New Comment, in the Comments group

3 Your username is shown, but you can delete this if you wish, then add your comments

4 Format the text, if desired, and then click outside the comment box to finish

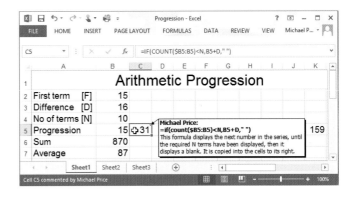

5 The presence of a comment is indicated by the red flash at the top right of the cell, and the comment box appears when you move the mouse over the cell

6 The Edit Comment command replaces the New Comment command, when the selected cell contains an existing comment

5 Excel Tables

The Excel table structure helps you to keep sets of data separate, so that you don't accidentally change other data when you are inserting or deleting rows and columns. There are other benefits also, such as structured cell references, automatic filters, sorts, and subtotals.

Create an Excel Table

Hot tip

In an Excel Table, the rows and columns are managed independently from the data in other rows and columns on the worksheet. In previous releases of Excel, this feature was called an Excel list.

To make it easier to manage and analyze a group of related data, you can turn a range of cells into an Excel Table. The range should contain no empty rows or empty columns.

To illustrate this feature, a table is used to interpret the genre (music classification) codes contained in the MP3 tags for music files (see page 40). This field often appears as a genre code such as (2) for country music, or (4) for disco.

Search on the Internet for ID3 genre code table, and select a suitable web page. There is a useful table, for example, at **www. gnu.org.ua/software/idest/manual/html_section/Genre-Codes. html**

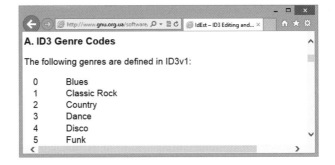

1 Select the table in Internet Explorer, and press Ctrl + C

2 Open the Music_List worksheet, locate two columns near the existing data, and type headers GenreID# and Genre

3 Select the second cell in the first of those columns then press Ctrl + V to copy the code table into the worksheet

Beware

The genre code is contained in brackets, and the value will therefore be treated as a negative number when the data is imported to an Excel worksheet.

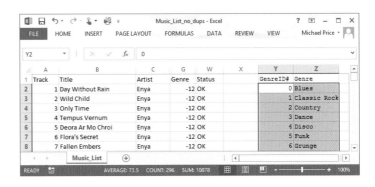

4 With the data and headers selected, click the Insert tab, then click Table in the Tables group

5 Check that the appropriate range of data is selected

6 If the first row has headers, select My table has headers, otherwise you'd let Excel generate default headers

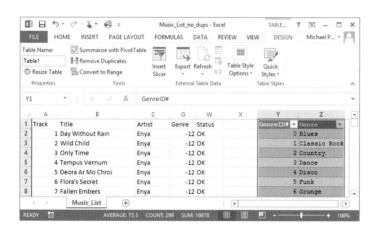

The table is given the default banding style, and Filter boxes are automatically added in the header row of each column, allowing you to sort or filter the contents.

The table will be given a default name, such as Table1. To change this name:

1 Click in the table, and click the Design tab

2 Click the Table Name box in the Properties group, to highlight the name

3 Type a new name for the table, Code for example, and press Enter to apply the change (and update all references to the old table name)

Don't forget

It may be best to remove worksheet protection and unfreeze panes, before you insert the new data.

Don't forget

If you click in the table, the context-sensitive Table Tools and Design tabs are displayed, so that you can customize or edit the table.

73

Hot tip

You can also change the names of tables, using the Name Manager on the Formulas tab (see page 63).

Edit Tables

1 Select the Music data and click Table on the Insert tab, to create another table, and change its name to Music

2 Click in any column in the Music table that is not required, then select Home, click the arrow next to Delete in the Cells group, and choose Delete Table Columns

3 Go to the end of the Code table, click in the last cell and select Home, Insert, Insert Table Row (or press Tab)

4 Type an entry, such as 148, New, then add another row with 149, New and another with 255, Other

5 Select the cells with values 148 and 149, then select the Home tab, and choose Delete, Delete Table Rows

You'll find that inserting or deleting rows and columns in one table will not affect the other tables in the worksheet.

Table Styles

The Design tab provides options to change the formatting of the rows and columns in the table.

① Specify if there's a header row, and turn banding on or off, using settings in the Table Style Options group

② Click the Quick Styles button, in the Table Styles group, to view the full list of styles

③ The styles selection bar is displayed, if there's room on the ribbon, and you can scroll the styles, or press the More button to show the full list

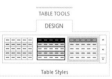

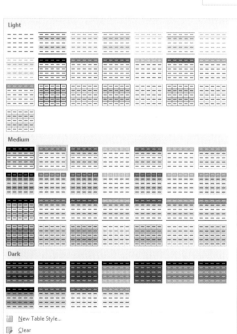

④ Make changes to the Table Style Options, and the new effects are incorporated into the Styles Selection panel

Table Totals

You can add a Totals row at the end of the table, and display the totals for columns (or use another function appropriate to the type of information stored in the column).

 1 Click in the table, select the Design tab, and click the Total Row box in the Table Style Options group

2 The Totals row is added as the last row of the table, and the last column (BitRate) is given a Total

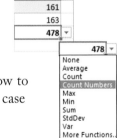

 Hot tip

The Subtotal function is inserted, with a number to indicate the operation:

101	AVERAGE
102	COUNT
103	COUNTA
104	MAX
105	MIN
106	PRODUCT
107	STDEV
108	STDEVP
109	SUM
110	VAR
111	VARP

Subtotal uses structured references to the table (see page 78).

3 Select the Total cell, and click the arrow to see the Total function applied (in this case the function used is Count Numbers)

4 You can apply a Total to any column. For Title, Comment, and FilePath, use Count. For FileSize use Average. For Length, use Sum, and for Year, use Min or Max

The More Functions option allows any Excel function to be used for computing the total for that column.

Count Unique Entries

For Artist and Album, you can count all unique entries, to give the numbers of individual artists and albums stored in the table:

1 Click in the Total cell for the Artist column, and begin typing the function =sum(1/countif(

2 Click the Artist header, to extend the formula

3 Type a comma, click the Artist header again, and then type two closing parentheses

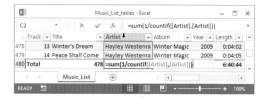

4 This is an array formula, so press Shift + Ctrl + Enter (rather than just Enter), and the count will be displayed

Hot tip

This calculates the frequency for each entry, inverts these counts, and sums up the resulting fractions. For example, if an entry appears three times, you get 1/3 + 1/3 + 1/3 for that entry, giving a count of 1. Each unique entry adds another 1.

Beware

This method of counting the number of duplicate entries assumes that there are no empty cells in the range being checked.

77

Don't forget

Use a similar formula to count the number of unique entries in the Album column.

{=SUM(1/COUNTIF([Album],[Album]))}		
Artist	Album	Year
Hayley Westenra	Winter Magic	2009
Hayley Westenra	Winter Magic	2009
18	40	1975

Structured References

The formulas shown for the totals illustrate the use of structured references. These allow you to refer to the contents of a table, using meaningful names, without having to be concerned about the specific row numbers and column letters, or changes that are caused when rows and columns are added or deleted. The structured references use the table name and column specifiers:

=Music	The table data	A2: K479
=Music[Length]	All the data in the Length column	F2:F479

You can add a special item specifier, to refer to particular parts:

=Music[#All]	The entire table, with headers, data and totals	A1:K480
=Music[#Data]	The table data	A2:K479
=Music[#Headers]	The header row	A1:K1
=Music[#Totals]	The totals row	A480:K480
=[@Length]	The intersection of the named column with the active row (n)	Fn

For formulas within the table, such as subtotals on the Totals row, you can leave off the table name. This forms an unqualified structured reference, e.g. [Bitrate]. However, outside the table, you need the fully qualified structured reference, e.g. Music[Bitrate].

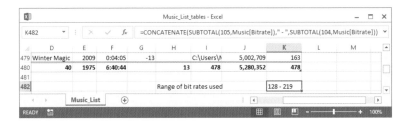

This formula includes two subtotal functions (see page 76) to obtain the minimum and the maximum values from the Bitrate column. The results are separated by a hyphen, and the three items are concatenated (joined), to form a single text string. This is displayed in the cell K334, which contains the formula.

Calculated Columns

You can add a calculated column to an Excel table. This uses a single formula that adjusts for each row, automatically expanding to include additional rows.

Start by inserting a new column in the table.

1 Click the end column (Bitrate), select the Home tab, and click the arrow next to Insert, which is found in the Cells group

2 Click Insert Table Columns to the Right, and then rename the new column as Style (i.e. music style)

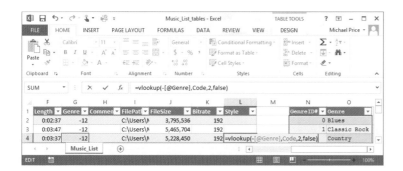

3 Click anywhere in the Style column and type a formula e.g. =vlookup(-[@Genre],Code,2,false) then press Enter

4 The formula that you type is automatically filled into all cells of the column, above as well as below the active cell

Don't forget

You need to enter the formula only once, and you won't need to use the Fill or Copy command when the table grows.

Hot tip

The formula in this example is a vertical table lookup. It matches the value from the Genre column with an entry in the first column of the Code table. It copies the associated text from the second column into the Styles column. See page 90 for an example of an hlookup (a horizontal lookup).

Insert Rows

1 Scroll to the last cell in the table, press Tab to add a new row, you'll see that the new formula is replicated

2 To add data from a text file (see page 42), click a cell in an empty part of the worksheet and select From Text (on the Data tab in the Get External Data group)

3 Locate and double-click the data file, then use the Text Import Wizard to specify the structure of the data file

4 When the wizard completes the review, confirm the temporary location for storing the data in the worksheet

5 Highlight the new data (excluding the header row), select the Home tab, and click Copy from the Clipboard group

6 Select the first cell in the new row added to the table then click Paste, from the Clipboard group

7 Additional rows are inserted into the table as necessary, to hold the new data records

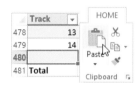

Microsoft Excel

This table inserted rows into your worksheet. This may cause data in cells below the table to shift down.

☐ Do not display this dialog again

OK

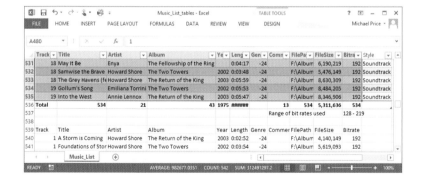

8 The data rows are copied into the extended table

9 The Totals are automatically adjusted, and you'll see that Style, the calculated column, is extended and updated to display values for the new data rows

Custom Sort

When new rows are inserted, it may be appropriate to sort the table, to position the new rows where they belong.

1. Click in the table, select the Home tab, click Sort & Filter, in the Editing group, and select Custom Sort

Or

Click in the table, select the Data tab, and click Sort, in the Sort & Filter group

2. The first time, there are no criteria defined, so click the arrow in "Sort by" to add a header, e.g. Artist

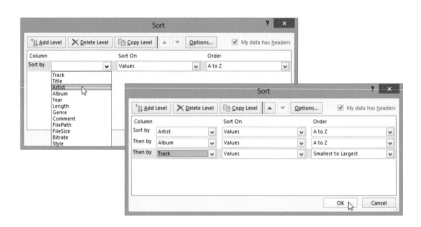

3. Click the Add Level button, choose a second header (e.g. Album), and then add a third level (Track) and click OK

Print a Table

You can print a table without having to select the print area explicitly (see page 32).

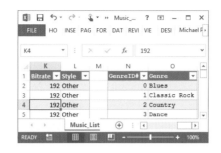

1 Select any cell in the table to activate it

2 Use Filters to restrict the display and print, for example, music for a specific Artist

3 Press the File tab, and then select Print (or press the shortcut key Ctrl + P)

4 For Settings, choose Print Selected Table, then adjust the paper size and scaling, if needed

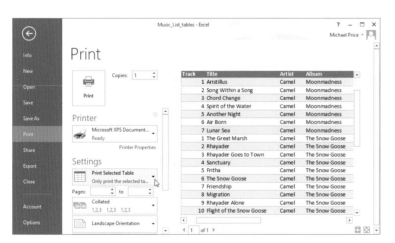

5 Specify the number of copies required, then click the Print button to complete the process

Print

Hot tip

You may wish to change to a different table style, one more suitable for printing (or select None for a plain effect).

Table Styles

Don't forget

You can print the active worksheet, the entire workbook, the selected data, or the active table.

	Print Active Sheets Only print the active sheets
	Print Entire Workbook Print the entire workbook
	Print Selection Only print the current selection
	Print Selected Table Only print the selected table

Ignore Print Area

Beware

Subtotals will be adjusted to match the filtered results. However, some formulas on the Totals row may continue to reference the whole of the table contents.

Summarize a Table

You can summarize the data, using the PivotTable feature. See page 165 for another example.

Select Insert and click Recommended PivotTables to see the suggestions that Excel 2013 makes for the data that is in your worksheets.

1 Click in the table, select the Insert tab, and then click the PivotTable button, in the Tables group

2 Choose the location for the PivotTable report, either a new worksheet or an empty portion of the current worksheet, e.g. A550, and then click OK

3 An empty PivotTable report is added at that location

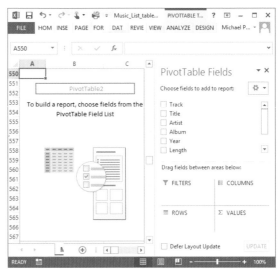

Hot tip

Click the Collapse Dialog box, select the first cell of the location, and then click the Expand Dialog box.

Don't forget

By default, text fields are added to the Row Labels area, and fields containing numbers are added to the Values area.

4 Click the boxes to select fields from the Field List (for example, Artist, Album, Track, and Length)

5 Rearrange the fields by clicking and dragging, or right-click a name and select the area where it should appear

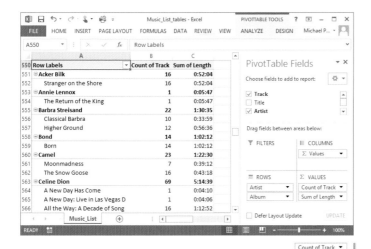

6 Click a numeric field in the Values list to reposition, move to a different area, or change value field settings

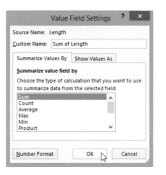

7 Choose how to summarize the values (e.g. sum, count, or average them)

8 Click the Number Format button, to change the way that a numeric value is displayed

9 When you select a PivotTable, Analyze and Design tabs for the associated tools will be added to the Ribbon

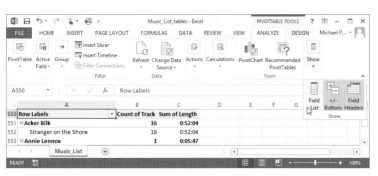

Convert to a Range

Hot tip

If you have just created a table from a range of data (see page 72), you can switch back to the range form by clicking Undo on the Quick Access toolbar.

You can turn an Excel table back into a range of data.

1 Click in the table to display the Table Tools entry on the ribbon

2 Select the Design tab, then click Convert to Range in the Tools group

3 Click Yes, to confirm that you do want to convert the table to a data range

4 The cell styles will be preserved, but the filter boxes will be removed from the headers

Don't forget

To remove the table style from the cells, select all the data, click the Home tab, click the down-arrow next to Cell Styles, in the Styles group, and choose the Normal style.

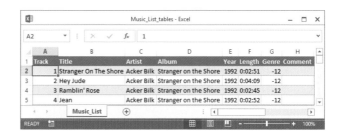

5 The Totals row will still appear, but all references will now be standard $A$1-style absolute cell references

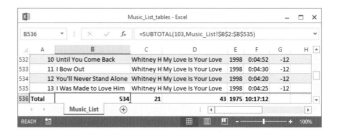

6 If you convert the range into a table again, you will need to recreate the structured reference formulas for the Totals row and the calculated columns

6 Advanced Functions

There is a large library of functions. To help locate the ones you want, related functions are grouped by category, and there's a Recently Used list. More functions are provided via Excel Add-ins. With nested functions in your formulas, use the Evaluate command to see how they work.

Function Library

1 Select the Formulas tab to see the Function Library group, with a Ribbon style that depends on window size

The function Library continues to expand, from a total of 320 in Excel 2007 and 400 in Excel 2010 to the current 450 in Excel 2013.

This starts with the Insert Function command, which allows you to enter keywords to search for a function (see page 66). It provides the syntax and a brief description for any function that you select, plus a link to more detailed help. Alternatively, you can select from one of the categories.

2 Click a Category command for an alphabetical list of the names of the functions that are included

The categories, and the number of functions included in each, are:

AutoSum	5	More Functions:		
Recently Used	10	Statistical	104
Financial	49	Engineering	54
Logical	9	Cube	7
Text	27	Information	20
Date & Time	24	Compatibility	40
Lookup & Ref	19	Web	4
Math & Trig	74		

AutoSum
AutoSum (introduced on page 68) provides quick access to functions (Sum, Average, Count, Min and Max) that are likely to be the most frequently used functions in many workbooks.

Recently Used
Recently Used remembers the functions you last used, allowing you to make repeated use of functions with the minimum of fuss, and without having to remember their particular categories.

Don't forget

AutoSum and Recently Used are the only categories that include duplicates of functions.

Logical Functions

Sometimes the value for one cell depends on the value in another cell. For example, test scores could be used to set grade levels.

1 The formula in C2 is =B2>=50 and gives the result True or False, depending on the value in B2

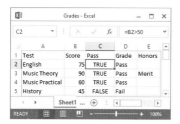

2 To display the more meaningful Pass or Fail, you'd use an IF formula, such as in D2, with =IF(B2>=50,"Pass","Fail")

3 Sometimes you need to check two conditions, e.g. in the E3 formula =IF(AND(B3>=50,B4>=50),"Merit","n/a")

The IF functions can be nested, with the False value being replaced by another IF function, to make a further test.

1 This formula gives the country code, if the name matches, or goes on to test for the next country name in the list

Hot tip

Comparisons (e.g. using the <, =, or > operators) that are either True or False are the basis of logical functions.

Don't forget

The AND function includes a set of logical tests, all of which must be True, to give a True result.

Hot tip

You could use an OR function for the first two countries here, since a match for either would give the same code.

Lookup/Reference Functions

If you have a number of items to check against, set up a list.

1 This example uses a list of country names (in alphabetical order), with their country codes stored in rows D1:IF2

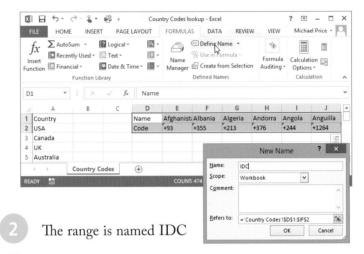

2 The range is named IDC

3 The lookup function requires the value, the lookup range, and the row number for the result (in this case row 2)

4 Copy the formula down, to look up the codes for the other countries

5 A mistype of Andorra results in #N/A, indicating that no match could be found

To reverse the process, and replace a number with a text value, you could use the CHOOSE function. For example:

1 To convert the value in cell B2 into a Rank, enter
=CHOOSE(B2,"First","Second","Third","Fourth","Fifth")

2 Copy the formula across to rank cells C2 to F2

3 To apply a suffix to the position value, use the formula
=B2&CHOOSE(B2,"st","nd","rd","th","th")

91

4 Copy the formula across to rank cells C2 to F2

You could store the values in a range of cells, but you must list the relevant cells individually in the formula.

You should use absolute cell references for the list of values, so that you can copy the formula without changing the references.

Financial Functions

Excel includes specialized functions for dealing with investments, securities, loans, and other financial transactions. For example, to calculate the monthly payments required for a mortgage, you'd use the PMT function. To illustrate, assume a purchase price of $250,000, interest at 6% per annum, and a 30-year period:

1 Enter the initial information into a worksheet, then, for the payment, begin typing the function =PMT(

2 Click the Insert Function button, to display the input form for the function arguments

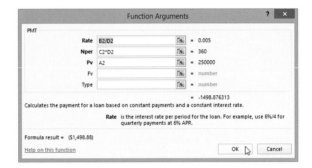

3 In the Rate box, enter the interest rate per payment period B2/D2 (i.e. 6%/12). In the Nper box, enter C2*D2 (30*12). In the PV box, enter A2 ($250,000). Click OK

The monthly payment required is displayed.

Perhaps you'd like to know what would happen if you paid the mortgage off over a shorter period:

1 Select the existing values and calculation, then drag down, using the Fill handle, to replicate into three more rows

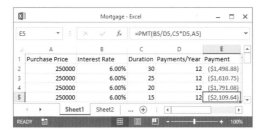

2 Change the duration to 25, 20 and 15 years, on successive rows, and observe the revised monthly payments required

3 Add a column, to show total interest paid, and enter the cumulative interest function =CUMIPMT(

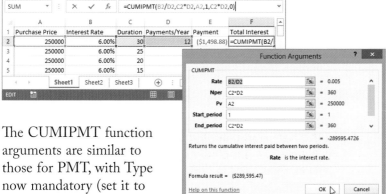

The CUMIPMT function arguments are similar to those for PMT, with Type now mandatory (set it to 0, for payment at end of month). The result shows how much interest would be paid out.

Copy the formula down, to see the cumulative interest for the other loan durations.

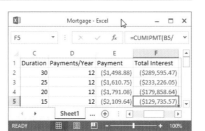

Date & Time Functions

Date and time values (see page 59) are numbers, and count the days since the starting point (usually January 1st, 1900). However, they can be displayed in various date or time formats.

 The whole-number portion of the value converts into month, day, and year (with account taken for leap years)

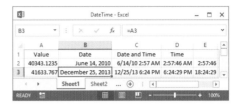

 The decimal portion indicates the time of day, so .123 is 2:57, and .767 is 6:24PM (or 18:24 on the 24-hour clock)

Date and Time Calculations

 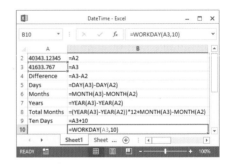

B4	Difference in days
B5	Subtracts calendar day numbers (may be minus)
B6	Subtracts calendar months (may be minus)
B7	Difference in years (ignores the part year)
B8	Twelve months for every year +/- the difference in months
B9	Adding ten days to A3 gives Jan 4, 2014
B10	Adding ten work days (to allow for weekends and holidays) gives the later date Jan 8, 2014

There's a worksheet function called DateDif that's not listed in the Date & Time category, or shown in Excel Help. The syntax is:

=DATEDIF(StartDate,EndDate,Interval)

The Interval code controls the result the function produces:

Hot tip

Excel's Visual Basic for Applications (VBA) has a similar function called DateDiff, but without the "ym", "yd", and "md" Interval parameters.

Interval value	Calculates the number between the dates of
"y"	Whole years
"m"	Whole months
"d"	Days in total
"ym"	Whole months, ignoring the years
"yd"	Days, ignoring the years
"md"	Days, ignoring the months and years

When entering the Interval code into DateDif as a constant, you enclose it in quotes. However, if your interval code is stored in a worksheet cell, it should not be enclosed in quotes in the cell.

1 Use the DateDif function with each of these codes in turn, to calculate the difference between the dates that are stored in cells B15 and B16

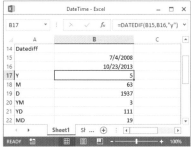

2 This function becomes useful when you need to calculate someone's exact age, in years, months, and days. For example, DateDif applied to the date of birth and the current date gives the following result:

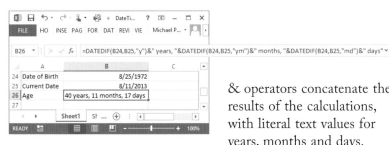

& operators concatenate the results of the calculations, with literal text values for years, months and days.

Hot tip

DateDif is applied three times, to obtain the years, months, and days, and the results are joined together into a single statement.

Text Functions

Values can be presented in many different ways, even though they remain stored as numbers. Sometimes, however, you actually want to convert the values into text (enclosed in quotes), perhaps to include them in a specific format, in a report or message.

This uses the Text function. Its syntax is =TEXT(value, format).

1 Format a number as text, with a fixed number of decimal places, with a comma as the thousands separator, if desired

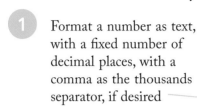

2 Display a number in money format, using any currency symbol

3 Display a number using the default currency for your system

4 Show the day of the week, for a date value, using the long or short form of the day name

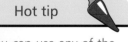
5 For examples of the number formats, choose the Custom category, in the Format Cells dialog, and scroll the list

There are several functions provided to help you manipulate a piece of text, to make it more suitable for presentation.

1 Remove all extraneous blanks, leaving a single space between words

2 Convert all the characters in the text into lower-case format

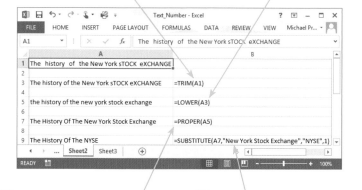

3 Convert all the text to proper case (title case)

4 Replace part of the text with different words

Excel does not have a Word Count function, but the text functions can be used in combination, to find the number of words in a cell.

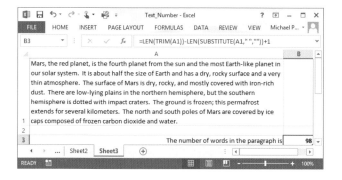

The Trim function removes multiple spaces from the text, then the first Len function counts all the characters, including spaces. The Substitute function removes all spaces from the text, then the second Len function counts the remaining characters. The difference between the two lengths is the number of spaces between words. Add one, and you will then have the number of words in the cell.

Math & Trig Functions

These functions allow you to carry out calculations, using cell contents, computed values, and constants. For example:

1. The Product function multiplies price times (1 - discount) quantity to get the cost of the item

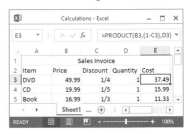

2. Copy the formula, to calculate the costs for the other items

3. The total cost is the sum of the individual item costs

You may sometimes want to make calculations without showing all of the intermediate values. For example:

1. The total cost (before discount) is the sum of the products of the item prices and item quantities, i.e. B3*D3 + B4*D4 + ...

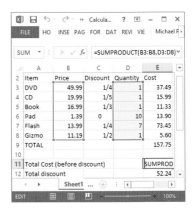

2. This value is calculated with the Sumproduct function, which multiplies the sets of cells and totals the results

3. Rather than using the Sumproduct function to calculate the total discount, you can simply subtract actual cost from total cost. This avoids problems with rounding errors, which

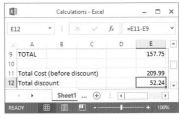

can show up in even straightforward functions, such as Sum

To illustrate the type of problem that can arise, imagine placing an order for goods where there's a special gift offered for spending $140 or more.

1. A quick check seems to indicate that the total is just over the amount required

2. But that the total that Excel actually calculates appears to be just under that amount

Excel hasn't got its sums wrong – the stored numbers that it totals aren't quite the same as those on display.

3. Change the cell format, to show more decimal places, and you'll see the actual values are slightly lower than those shown

```
33.326667
13.326667
11.326667
9.266667
65.286667
7.460000
139.993333
```

4. Click cell E3, and then add the Round function to the existing formula, to round the item cost to two places

5. Copy the formula into cells E4:E8, and you'll see that the total is now the expected amount, qualifying for the gift

The Round function rounds up or down. So 1.234 becomes 1.23, while 1.236 becomes 1.24 (rounded to two decimal places). You can specify a negative number of places, to round the values to the nearest multiple of ten (-1 places) or of one hundred (-2 places), etc.

```
33.330000
13.330000
11.330000
9.270000
65.290000
7.460000
140.010000
```

Hot tip

Values may be displayed, or converted to text, with a fixed number of decimal digits, but the original value will still have the same number of digits as originally typed, or as calculated when the value was created.

Beware

You will find that what you see on the worksheet isn't always what you get in the calculations.

Don't forget

In some cases, you may always want to round the values in the same direction. Excel provides the functions Roundup and Rounddown for those situations.

Random Numbers

It is sometimes useful to produce sets of random numbers. This could be for sample data, when creating or testing worksheets. Another use might be to select a variety of tracks from your music library, to generate a play list.

1 Click A1, and enter the function =Rand(), to generate a random number between 0 and 1

2 Copy A1 down into A2:A5, and a different number will be shown in each cell

3 Click C1 and enter function =Randbetween(1,+10), which generates a whole number less than or equal to 10

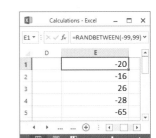

4 Copy B1 down into B2:B5, and a number will be shown in each cell (with possible repeats, since there are only ten possibilities)

5 You can generate negative numbers: for example, E1:E5 has values between -99 and +99

6 Select the Formulas tab then click Calculate Now in the Calculation group, and the numbers will be regenerated

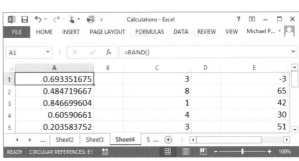

Other Functions: Statistical

There's a large number of statistical functions, but the most likely one to be used is the Average function.

1 Create a block A1:E5 of random numbers between 101 and 200, to use as data for the functions

	A	B	C	D	E
1	139	147	135	128	123
2	125	128	126	174	115
3	177	163	126	113	110
4	162	185	158	124	189
5	169	126	121	120	108

A1 · : × ✓ ƒx =RANDBETWEEN(101,120)

Stats - Excel

Sheet1

2 Define the name Sample for the range $A$1:$A$5

3 Select and Copy A1:E5, then select the Home tab, click the arrow on the Paste command, and select Paste Values (to replace the formula with the literal value, in each cell)

Calculate some typical statistics.

1 The arithmetic mean is =Average(Sample)

2 The number in the middle of the sample is =Median(Sample)

	A	B	C	D	E
1	139	147	135	128	123
2	125	128	126	174	115
3	177	163	126	113	110
4	162	185	158	124	189
5	169	126	121	120	108
6					
7		=AVERAGE(Sample)			139.64
8		=MEDIAN(Sample)			128
9		=MODE(Sample)			126
10		=COUNT(Sample)			25
11		=COUNTIF(Sample,">=150")			8
12		=MAX(Sample)			189
13		=MIN(Sample)			108

A1 · : × ✓ ƒx 139

Stats - Excel

Sheet1

3 The most frequently occurring value is =Mode(Sample)

4 The number of values in the sample is =Count(Sample)

5 The number of values in the sample that are greater than or equal to 150 is =Countif(Sample,">=150")

6 The maximum value in the sample is =Max(Sample)

7 The minimum value in the sample is =Min(Sample)

Hot tip

Use Copy, Paste Special, Paste Values, to replace the formulas, so that the set of random numbers generated won't later be affected by recalculation of the worksheet.

Don't forget

There are a number of different ways to interpret the term Average. Make sure that you use the function that's appropriate for your requirements.

Other Functions: Engineering

There are some rather esoteric functions in the Engineering category, but some are quite generally applicable, for example:

 Convert from one measurement system to another, using the function =Convert(value, from_unit, to_unit)

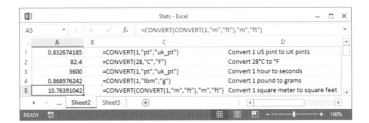

This function deals with units of weight and mass, distance, time, pressure, force, energy, power, magnetism, temperature, and liquids.

There are functions to convert between any two pairs of number systems, including binary, decimal, hexadecimal, and octal.

 Convert decimal values to their binary, octal, and hexadecimal equivalents

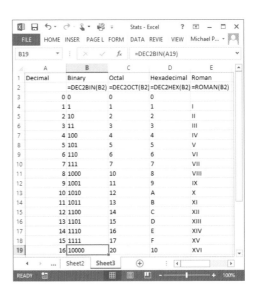

=ROMAN(1499,0)	MCDXCIX
=ROMAN(1499,1)	MLDVLIV
=ROMAN(1499,2)	MXDIX
=ROMAN(1499,3)	MVDIV
=ROMAN(1499,4)	MID

There's also a Roman numeral conversion, but it's just a one-way conversion between Arabic numerals and Roman numerals (and it comes from the Math & Trig category, rather than Engineering).

Excel Add-ins

There are Add-ins included with Excel, but they must be loaded before they can be used.

1 Click the File tab, and then click the Options button

2 Click the Add-Ins category, and, in the Manage box, click Excel Add-ins, and then click Go

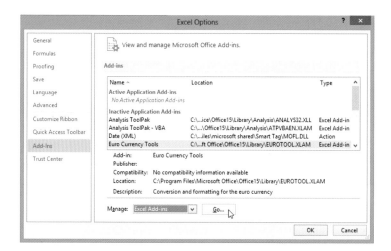

3 To load the Excel Add-in, select the associated check-box, and then click OK

4 You may be prompted to install some of the add-in programs that you select

5 The new functions can be found on the Formulas tab Solutions group, or on the Data tab Analysis group

Hot tip

If you are still looking for the functions you need, you may find them in an Excel Add-in, such as the Analysis ToolPak or the Solver Add-in.

103

Don't forget

To unload an Excel Add-in, clear the associated check-box, and then click OK. This does not delete the Add-in from your computer.

Evaluate Formula

If you are not sure exactly how a formula works, especially when there are nested functions, use the Evaluate command to run the formula one step at a time.

1 Select the cell with the formula you wish to investigate

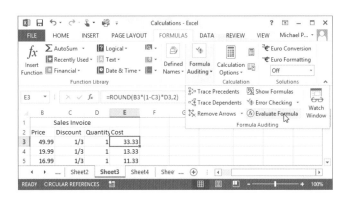

Hot tip

This is the formula for rounding the item costs, as shown in step 4 on page 99.

2 Select the Formulas tab, click the Formula Auditing button, and then select the Evaluate Formula command

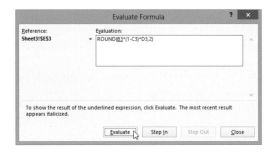

Don't forget

Press the Step In button, to check details like the value of a constant, or to see the expansion of range or table names.

Click Step Out to carry on with the evaluation.

Click Restart, or Finish.

3 Press the Evaluate button, to move the calculation on a step, then press again to move to the subsequent steps

4 The expressions in the formula are calculated in turn

5 The intermediate values are displayed

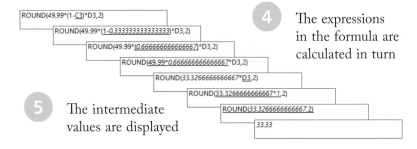

7 Control Excel

To keep control of your worksheets, audit the formulas, and check for errors. Make backup copies, and use the automatic save and recover capabilities. You can also control Excel through startup switches, shortcuts, KeyTips for the Ribbon commands, the Quick Access and Mini toolbars.

Audit Formulas

1. Click the Formulas tab, to see the Formula Auditing group

2. If the commands are grayed, click the File tab, select Excel Options, and then click Advanced

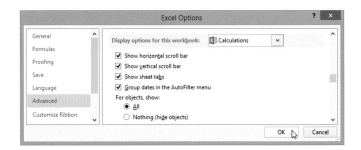

3. In the Display options for this Workbook section, make sure that the All option is selected

4. Select a cell, and click the Trace Precedents button in the Formula Auditing group

5. With cells where there is no formula, such as B3, you receive a message

6. With cells, that contain a formula, such as E9, the arrow and box show the cells that are directly referred to by that formula

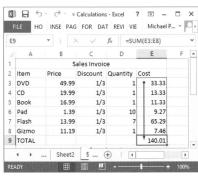

7 Click Trace Precedents, to see the next level of cells (if the first level of precedent cells refer to more cells)

8 Click the Trace Dependents button, to show the cells that rely on the value in the selected cell

9 Click the Remove Arrows button, in Formula Auditing

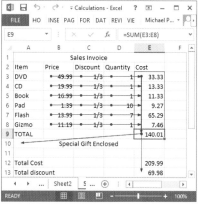

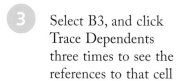

You can analyze the role of cells that contain only literal values:

1 Click a cell, e.g. B2, that contains no formula, and click Trace Dependents

2 If there are no cell references, you receive a warning message

3 Select B3, and click Trace Dependents three times to see the references to that cell

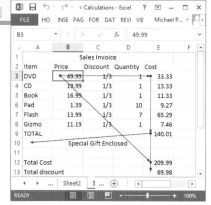

Protect Formulas

1 Click Show Formulas on the Formulas tab to display the formulas in the worksheet

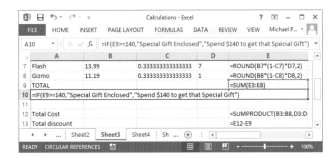

2 Click Show Formulas again to return to displaying the results of the formulas

3 To hide a formula, select the cell, then click the Home tab, Format, and Format Cells

4 Click in the box labeled Hidden, and then click OK

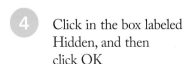

5 Select Protect Sheet from Home, Format (or from Review, Changes as suggested) then click OK

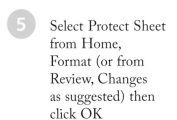

6 The formula will no longer display on the Formula bar when you select the cell. It is also hidden when you choose Show Formulas

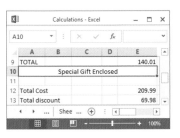

Check for Errors

Excel applies rules to check for potential errors in formulas.

1 Click the File tab, select Options, and then click Formulas

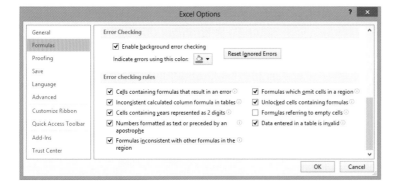

2 Select or clear the check-boxes, to change the errors that Excel will detect

3 Select Formulas, and click the arrow on Error Checking, in the Formula Auditing group

4 Click Error Checking, to review errors one by one, making corrections on the Formula bar

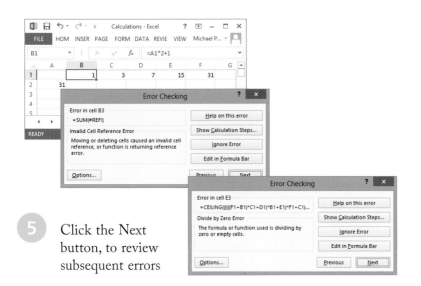

5 Click the Next button, to review subsequent errors

...cont'd

Hot tip

The Error Checking options become very useful when you have large worksheets, where errors and warnings are off screen and out of view.

You can also review individual errors on the worksheet.

1 Click an error, and then select Trace Error, from the Error Checking menu in Formula Auditing

2 You can select Circular References, to see the cells that refer to their own contents, directly or indirectly

3 Click a cell from the list, to navigate to that location

4 Press F9 to recalculate the worksheet, and the cells involved in circular references will be identified

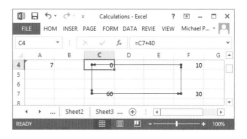

Don't forget

Click Trace Empty Cell, to identify the empty cells referred to, directly or indirectly, by the selected formula.

5 Click the Information button on an individual error, to see more options, which are tailored to the particular type of error being reviewed

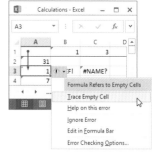

Backup

1 To make a copy of your workbook, click the File tab and select Open (or press the Ctrl + O shortcut key)

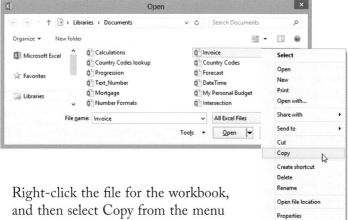

Hot tip

When you are working on a large worksheet, it is often helpful to make a copy before you apply significant changes, so that you can undo them, if necessary.

2 Right-click the file for the workbook, and then select Copy from the menu

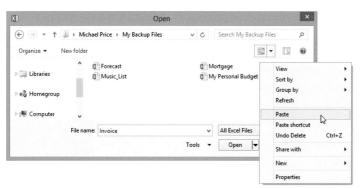

Hot tip

You can also keep extra copies of your workbooks in your SkyDrive (see page 180).

3 Switch to the backup folder, right-click an empty area, and then select Paste

4 The file is copied to the folder, unless there's an existing copy in the backup folder

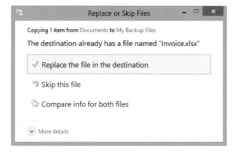

Don't forget

If there's already a copy, Windows compares the two versions, and lets you choose to replace the file or skip copying the workbook.

5 Compare file info to confirm which version you want

AutoSave and AutoRecover

To review and adjust the AutoRecover and AutoSave settings:

Click the File tab, then click Options, and select Save

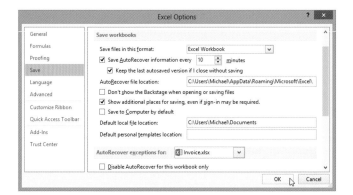

2 Make sure Save AutoRecover information box is checked, review the frequency then click OK to save any changes

If your system shuts down without saving the current changes, the next time you start up Windows and Excel, you'll be given the opportunity to recover your changes, as recorded up to the last AutoSave.

1 Select an entry, click the arrow and choose Open, Save As or Delete as appropriate

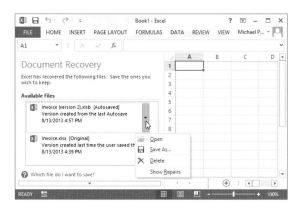

Hot tip

Excel will automatically save your worksheet, periodically, and can recover the file if your system shuts down in the middle of an update.

Don't forget

Excel will keep the last autosaved version, even when you deliberately close without saving, so you can still recover your latest changes.

Hot tip

The Document Recovery task pane displays up to three versions of your file, with the most recent at the top.

Startup Switches

When you start Excel in the usual way, it displays the Excel splash screen, and then opens the Excel start screen where you can select a new blank workbook, a recent workbook or a template.

Excel 2013 normally opens at the Excel Start screen, but you can bypass this if you wish.

To start Excel without these items displaying:

1 Press the Windows Logo key + R, type excel.exe /e, and then press Enter

Don't forget

You can use this method to start Excel in safe mode by typing excel.exe /safe. This can be useful if you are having problems opening a particular workbook.

2 Excel opens without the splash or start screen

Hot tip

You can create a shortcut to Excel, with your required parameters, and place this on the Desktop or the Taskbar.

3 Select the File tab to create or open a workbook

When you start Excel using the Start screen tile or the Taskbar icon, the Splash screen and Start screen will still be displayed.

Create a Shortcut

To create a shortcut to Excel:

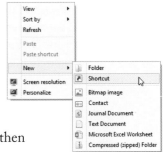

1 Locate the Excel.exe file on your hard drive, typically C:\Program Files\Microsoft Office\Office15\Excel.exe

2 Right-click the Desktop, and then select New, Shortcut

3 Browse to the Excel.exe file and select it, then add the required switch (e.g. /e or /safe) outside the quote marks

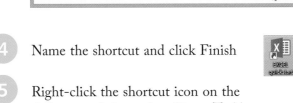

4 Name the shortcut and click Finish

5 Right-click the shortcut icon on the desktop, and then select Pin to Taskbar (or Pin to Start)

6 Select the entry, to launch the program, or right-click the entry to unpin it

Ribbon KeyTips

Although the Ribbon is designed for mouse and touch selection, it is still possible to carry out any task available on the Ribbon without moving your hands from the keyboard.

1   Press and release the Alt key (or press the F10 key) to show KeyTips (the keyboard shortcuts for the Ribbon)

2   Press the letter for the command tab that you want to display; for example, press W for View

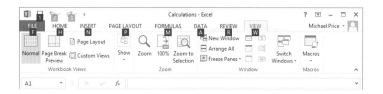

3   Press the letter(s) for the command or group that you want; for example, press ZS for Show/Hide

Hot tip

If you hold down the Alt key for a couple of seconds, the KeyTips will display. Click F10 to hide them, temporarily.

Don't forget

The KeyTips change when you select a tab, and further KeyTips display when you select specific commands.

Hot tip

It doesn't matter if Alt is pressed or not: the shortcut keys in the KeyTips will still operate. You can also use upper or lower case.

Using KeyTips

① To go to a specific cell, C7 for example, press these keys:

Alt

H

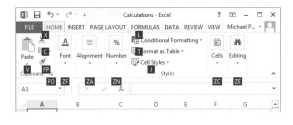

FD

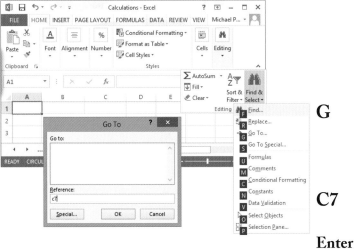

G

C7

Enter

② The active cell changes to C7, the cell address required

3 With C7 selected, to insert AutoSum, press these keys:

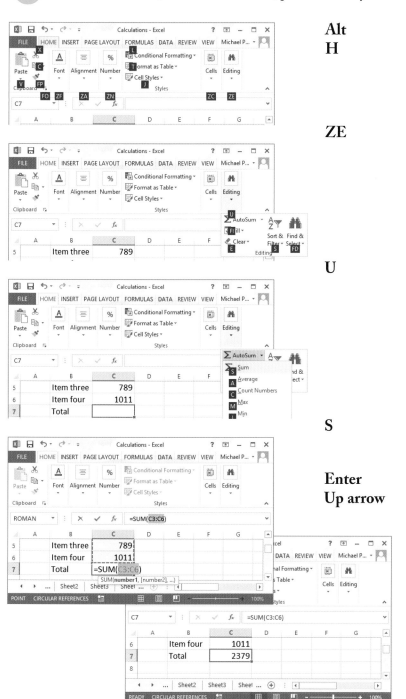

Alt
H

ZE

U

S

Enter
Up arrow

Hot tip

You can insert the AutoSum function into the active cell using keystrokes only.

Hot tip

ZE expands the Editing group, but you can bypass this and go straight to U (AutoSum) if you don't need the visual prompt.

Don't forget

For tasks that you perform often, the KeyTips option can become the quickest way to operate, as you become familiar with the keystrokes needed.

Collapse the Ribbon

1 Right-click the Ribbon, Tab bar or Quick Access bar and select Collapse the Ribbon, or click Ribbon Display Options and select Show Tabs

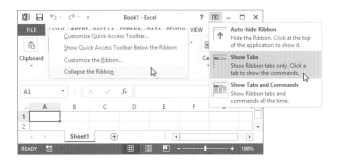

Hot tip

You can also double-click the current tab, press keys Ctrl + F1, or click the Collapse button at the corner of the Ribbon on the right.

2 With the Ribbon minimized, single-click a tab to display the Ribbon temporarily, to select commands from that tab

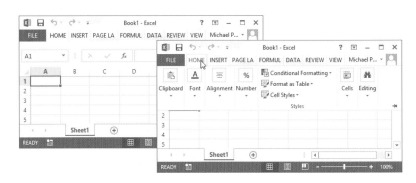

Don't forget

To redisplay the Ribbon, right-click again, reselect Collapse the Ribbon, or select Show Tabs and Commands. You can also click the Pin on the temporarily expanded Ribbon.

3 The Alt key and the KeyTips still operate, even when you have the Ribbon minimized

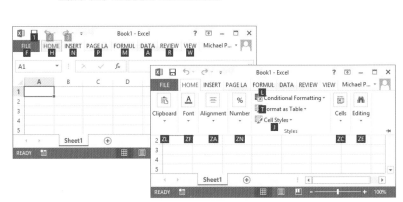

Hot tip

When you close down Excel with the Ribbon collapsed, it will still be collapsed when Excel restarts. When the Ribbon is fully displayed at close down, it will be displayed on restart.

Quick Access Toolbar

The Quick Access Toolbar contains a set of commands that are independent of the particular Command tab being displayed. Initially there are three commands (Save, Undo, and Redo) plus a Customize button, but you can add other commands. By default, the Quick Access Toolbar is located above the File tab, but you can move it below the Ribbon.

1 Right-click the Command tab bar, and select Show Quick Access Toolbar Below the Ribbon

2 To restore the default, right-click the Command tab bar, then select Show Quick Access Toolbar Above the Ribbon

3 To add a command, click Customize Quick Access Toolbar

4 Choose a command from the list, or select More Commands

5 Choose a command category, select a command, click Add then click OK to place that command on the toolbar

Mini Toolbar

The Mini toolbar appears when you select text, or when editing the contents of a cell (and also when working with charts and text boxes). It offers quick access to the tools you need for text editing, such as font, size, style, alignment, color, and bullets. To see the mini toolbar:

1 Choose a cell with text content, enter edit mode, by pressing F2, and then select (highlight) part of the text

2 The Mini toolbar appears very faintly, being almost completely transparent

3 Move the mouse pointer towards the Mini toolbar, and the image strengthens

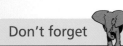

4 When the mouse pointer moves over the toolbar, the image solidifies and the toolbar is activated

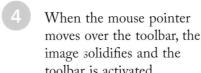

5 Move the mouse pointer away from the toolbar, and the image fades out and may disappear

This feature was created as an extension of the context (right-click) menu, and it may appear whenever that menu appears.

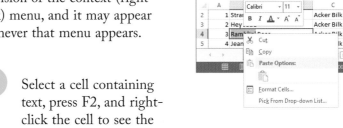

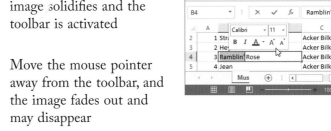

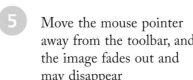

6 Select a cell containing text, press F2, and right-click the cell to see the Mini toolbar above the context menu

Print Worksheets

To preview printing for multiple worksheets:

1 Open the workbook, and click the tab for the first sheet

2 To select adjacent sheets, hold down the Shift key, and click the tab for the last sheet in the group

3 To add other, non-adjacent sheets, hold down the Ctrl key and click the tabs for all of the other sheets required

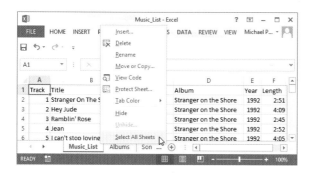

4 To select all the sheets, right-click any tab, then click Select All Sheets

5 Click the File tab, and select Print, for the Print Preview and the settings

Alternatively, press the keyboard shortcut Ctrl + F2

If you prefer to use KeyTips shortcuts, press Alt F P V

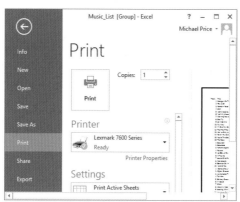

6 The Preview pane shows print previews for selected sheets

121

Beware

If you change any cell while multiple sheets are selected, the change is automatically applied to all selected sheets.

Don't forget

When multiple sheets are selected, the term [Group] appears on the Title bar.

To cancel the selection, click any unselected tab, or right-click any tab and click Ungroup Sheets.

...cont'd

Review the print preview before sending it to the printer.

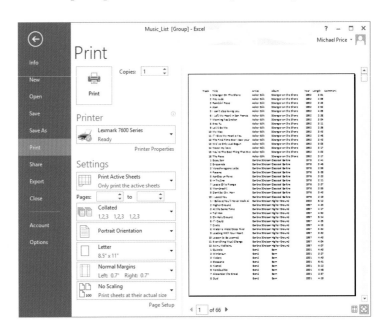

Hot tip

Click the Page Setup link to make detailed changes to the print settings. Click the Printer Properties link to control the printer.

Don't forget

If the settings are already correct, you can use the Quick Print button (see page 33) to start the Print, without previewing.

1. Click the Next Page arrow to go forward, or the Previous Page arrow to go back

2. Click the Show Margins button, to display margins, and click and drag the margins to adjust their positions

3. Click the Zoom to Page button to switch between close-up and full page views

4. Click the Settings buttons to adjust items, such as paper size, orientation, scaling, and collation

5. Click Printer button to select a printer other than the default

6. Click the Print button to start the printing

8 Charts

Excel makes it easy to turn your worksheet data into a chart. You can apply formatting, change the type, reselect the data, and add effects, such as 3-D display. Special chart types allow you to display data for stocks and shares. You can print the completed charts on their own, or as part of the worksheet.

Create a Chart

The following information about share purchases and prices will be used for the purpose of illustrating the Excel charting features.

1 Total value of shares in portfolio at start of each year (to be charted)

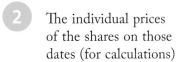 2 The individual prices of the shares on those dates (for calculations)

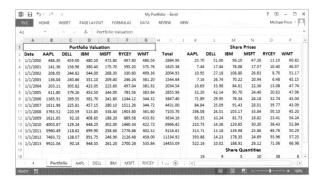

3 The total number of shares held (constants, for simplicity)

Select the Data

Some chart types, such as pie and bubble charts, require a specific data arrangement. For most chart types, however, including line, column, and bar charts, you can use the data as arranged in the rows or columns of the worksheet.

1 Select the cells that contain the data that you want to use for the chart (or click a cell and let Excel select the data)

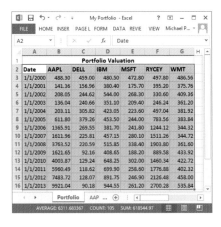

2 Click the Insert tab, and then select a chart type (Column for example) from the Charts group

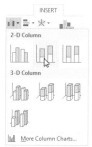

3 Choose the chart subtype, e.g. 2-D Stacked Column (to show how each share contributes to the total value)

4 The chart is superimposed over the data on the worksheet, and Chart Tools (Design, Layout, and Format tabs) are added to the Ribbon

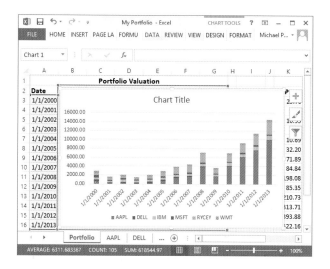

5 Click Move Chart, in the Location group on the Design tab, to choose where you want the chart to be placed. For example, choose New sheet to create a separate chart sheet with default name Chart1

125

Default Chart Type

Excel will recommend chart types for your selected data:

1 Click the Recommended Charts button (or click the arrow on the corner of the Charts group)

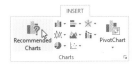

The Recommended Charts button lets you pick from a variety of charts that are right for your data.

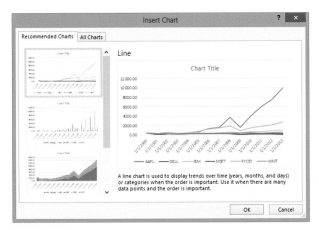

2 Click the All Charts tab to see the range of charts

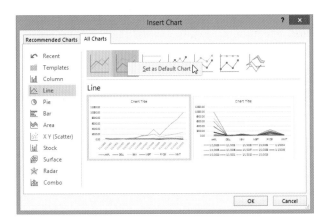

3 Right-click any chart type and select Set as Default Chart

4 With a data range selected, press F11 and the default chart type is displayed on a chart sheet, using the next free name (Chart2 in this case)

Change Chart Layout

127

Hot tip

You can select Quick Layout from Charts Layouts and try out the predefined sets of layout options to see if one of these suits you.

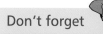

1 Select Chart Tools Design and click Add Chart Element from Chart Layouts group

2 Select Chart Title and choose the position, e.g. Above Chart

3 Right-click the sample words Chart Title, and select Edit Text, to amend the wording

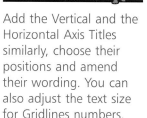

Don't forget

Add the Vertical and the Horizontal Axis Titles similarly, choose their positions and amend their wording. You can also adjust the text size for Gridlines numbers.

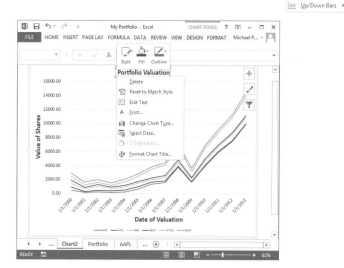

Hot tip

Instead of typing the titles directly, link to a cell on the worksheet. Click in the title, type = on the Formula bar, select the cell with the text, and then press Enter.

4 Right-click the text and select Font to adjust text styles

Legend and Data Table

Hot tip

The Legend provides the key to the entries on the chart. In this case, the stock symbols for all of the shares.

Hot tip

You can also display data labels, to show the data values at each point on the lines.

Don't forget

If you show the data for the chart in a table and include Legend keys, you can then select None to turn off display of the Legend itself.

1 Select Design, Add Chart Elements, Legend and choose its position (and alignment) on the chart, e.g. Right

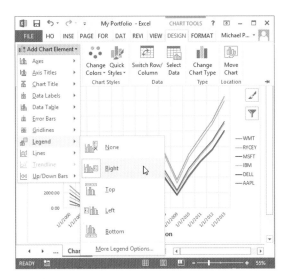

2 To show the full details. click Data Table, and choose where to position the table, and whether to display keys

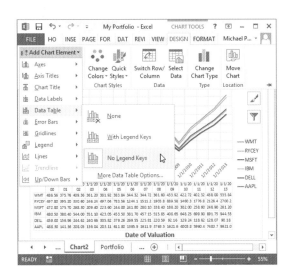

3 Again, you can adjust the text size and style for the entries in the Legend and the data table

Change Chart Type

1   Click the chart area, to display Chart Tools

2   Select the Design tab, and click Change Chart Type from the Type group

Hot tip

If you select your data and press F11 to insert the default chart type on the next chart sheet, you can then change the chart type and style.

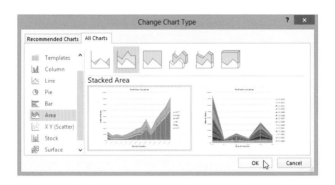

3   In the Change Chart Type dialog, select the chart type and subtype (for example, chart type Area and subtype Stacked Area), then click OK

4   Another way to compare the relative contributions of the shares is to use type Area and subtype 100% Stacked Area

Beware

When you change the chart style, you may need to reapply other changes, such as text font sizes.

5   The Design, Chart Styles group allows you to change the colors and the overall visual style for your chart

Pie Chart

1 Select the data labels and one set of data, in an adjacent row (or hold down Ctrl to select non-adjacent cells)

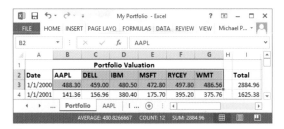

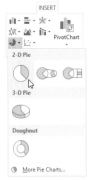

2 Click the Insert tab, select Pie from the Charts group, and choose the chart type, the standard 2-D Pie Chart for example

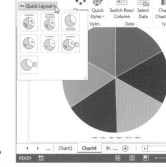

3 Click the Design tab, and select Move Chart, to create a chart sheet, Chart3 for example

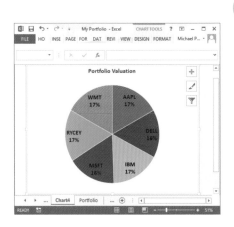

4 Select Quick Layout, in the Chart Layouts group, and choose one of the predefined layouts, which provide ways to handle the data labels, legend and titles

You can change the data series selected for the pie chart.

1 Select the Chart Tools Design tab, and then click Select Data, in the Data group

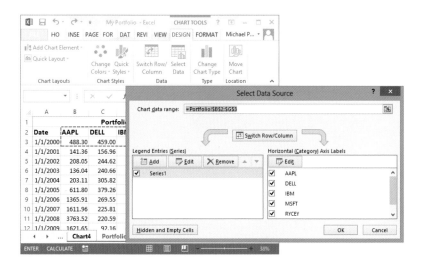

2 Click the data selection (usually Series1), and then click the Edit button

3 Click the Collapse button, and select a new range of data, such as the 1/1/2009 values, then click Expand

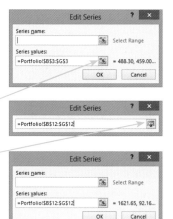

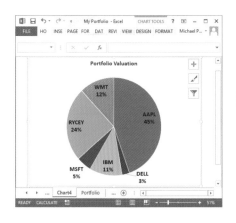

4 Click OK, and the set of data for the selected period will be displayed in the updated pie chart

3-D Pie Chart

One of the subtypes for the pie chart offers a 3-D view.

 Select the Chart Tools Design tab, click Change Chart Type, select Pie, 3-D Pie, and then click OK

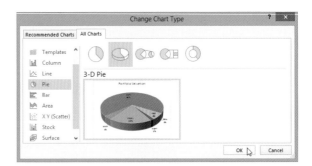

Don't forget

In a 3-D pie chart, it is the chart segments that are displayed in 3-D format, rather than the data itself (hence the grayed Z component).

 Right-click the chart, select 3-D Rotation, set rotation values (e.g. X: 270°, Y: 30°, Perspective: 15°), then click Close

Hot tip

Experiment with the rotation and format options, to find the most effective presentation form for your data.

The information is presented in 3-D display form. You can select Chart Tools Format to adjust the appearance, e.g. to add a background color

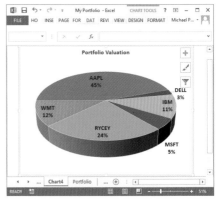

3-D Column Chart

A true 3-D chart has three sets of values to plot, giving three axes. In the example data, these would be Shares, Values, and Dates.

1 Select the data, click Insert, Charts, Column, and select the 3-D Column chart type

2 Select Chart Tools, Design and Format, to make the desired adjustments to the appearance. Right-click and select 3-D Rotation to change orientation and perspective

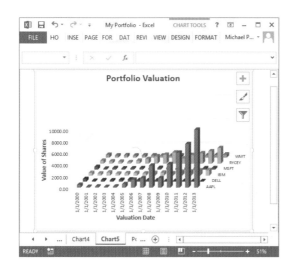

Share Price Data

The share prices in the portfolio worksheet were taken from price history tables downloaded from the Yahoo Finance website.

1 Go to **finance.yahoo.com**, search for the stock code, msft for example, then click the Historical Prices link

Don't forget

The price history table at Yahoo! Finance provides information in reverse date sequence, on a daily, weekly, or monthly basis. Use the Adjusted Close values to ensure that the prices are comparable over time.

2 Scroll down to the end of the list, and click Download to Spreadsheet

This provides a comma-separated file of dates, prices, and volumes for the selected share. The data can be sorted and converted into an Excel lookup table.

Hot tip

See page 72 for details on converting a range into an Excel table. See page 90 for an example of using the VLOOKUP function.

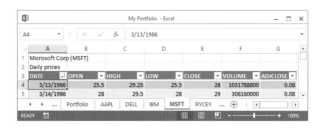

The Lookup table for each share is used to find the price of the share on particular dates.

Line Chart

The charts, so far, have used just a few dates from the tables. The complete tables, however, provide a continuous view of the data.

1 The Historical worksheet contains the date column and adjusted closing price column for each of the shares

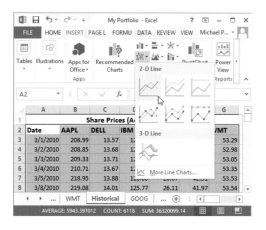

2 Select the data, click Insert, Chart and Line, then choose the 2-D Line chart subtype, to get a plot for each share

Hot tip

You can choose line, stacked line, or 100% stacked line (with or without markers). There's also a 3-D line, but this is just a perspective view, not three axes of data.

Don't forget

As with all the charts, you can move this chart to a separate chart sheet and adjust position and styles for the titles and the legend.

Stock Chart

The downloaded share data can also be used for a special type of chart, known as the Stock Chart.

 1 From the share table, filter the data (e.g. for 2012), and then select the columns for Date, High, Low, and Close

2 Open the Insert Chart dialog (see page 126), select the Stock charts, select type Open-High-Low-Close, and then click OK

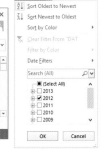

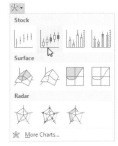

3 The prices are plotted, with lines for high/low, hollow boxes for increases, and solid boxes for decreases

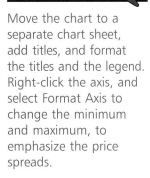

Mixed Types

You can have more than one type of chart displayed at the same time, as in the Volume subtypes of the stock chart.

1 Insert a table column after the Date column, and move the Volume column to that position

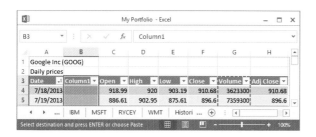

137

Hot tip

You need to rearrange the data downloaded from Yahoo! Finance, to create the volume stock charts, since volumes must be listed before the various share prices.

2 Select the data, including the headings, and Insert the Stock chart, choosing type Volume-Open-High-Low-Close

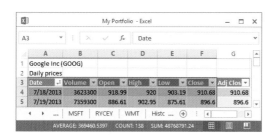

The chart uses two vertical axes, to show volume and price values.

Don't forget

In this example, the two types of chart use the same horizontal values (dates). When necessary, however, Excel will specify a secondary horizontal axis.

Print Charts

When you have an embedded chart in your worksheet, it prints as positioned, along with the data, when you select Print from the File tab, and click the Print button. To print the chart on its own:

1 Select the chart, then select the File tab and click Print

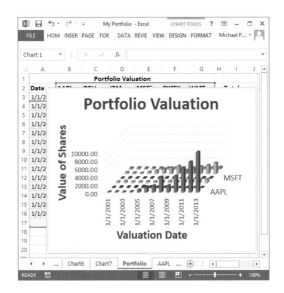

2 An extra "Print what" option (Selected Chart) appears, and the other options are grayed, so only the chart will print

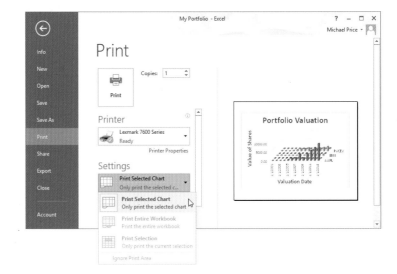

9 Macros in Excel

If there are tasks that you carry out frequently, you can define the actions required, as a macro. You can assign the macro to a key combination, or to an icon on the toolbar, to make it easy to reuse. However, you must make sure that security is in place to prevent abuse.

Macros

Any task in Excel may be performed by a macro. Macros are often used to carry out simple but repetitive tasks, such as entering your name and address, or inserting a standard piece of text. In other cases, macros may be used for complex and involved tasks, difficult to reproduce accurately without some kind of help.

To create a macro, carry out an example of the actions, with Excel recording the keystrokes involved as you complete the task. The sequence is stored as a macro, using Visual Basic for Applications programming language. You can edit your recorded macros, or create macros from scratch, using the Visual Basic Editor.

Macros can be very powerful, because they are able to run commands on your computer. For this reason, Microsoft Excel prevents the default Excel 2013 file format (file type .xlsx) from storing VBA macro code.

Therefore, the recommended place for storing the macros you create is in your hidden Personal Macro Workbook, and this is the method used for the examples in the following pages.

If you share macros, they need to be stored in the workbooks that use them. These workbooks must then be saved in the Excel 2013 macro-enabled file format (file type .xlsm). In such cases, you may need to reset the security level, temporarily, to enable all macros, so that you can work on macros in the active workbook:

Beware

Because macros have such a wide range of capabilities, they can be subject to misuse. Microsoft has included security checks and limitations in Excel, to authenticate macros, and to help prevent them being introduced into your system and run without your knowledge.

Don't forget

To check which type of workbook you have open, tell Windows to reveal the file type (see page 37).

Beware

Enable all macros is not recommended as a permanent setting. Select a more restricted level as soon as you have finished creating or changing the macros stored in your active workbook.

1 Select File tab, Options, Trust Center, then click the Trust Center Settings and select Macro Settings

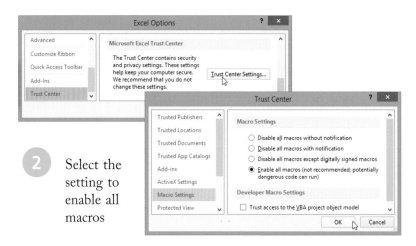

2 Select the setting to enable all macros

Create Macros

To display the commands for recording and viewing macros:

1 Select the View tab, and click the arrow below the Macros button, in the Macros group

2 You can choose to view or record macros, and choose between relative or absolute cell references (a toggle setting)

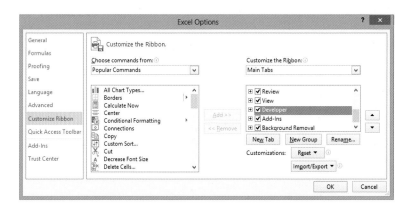

These options are also available from the Developer tab, along with the Macro Security and Visual Basic commands. By default, this tab is not displayed. To add the Developer tab to the Ribbon:

1 Click the File tab, and then select Options (or press the keys Alt F T) and choose Customize Ribbon

2 Click the Developer box, in the Main Tabs section, and the Developer tab will be added to the tab bar

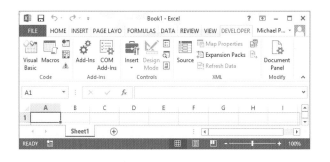

Record a Macro

Assume that you need to add some standard disclaimer text to a number of workbooks. To create a macro for this:

1 Open a blank workbook, and click in cell A1

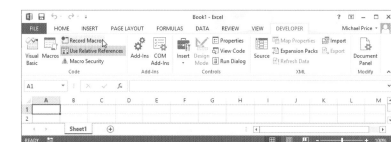

2 Select the Developer tab, then, from the Code group, click Use Relative References, and click Record Macro

3 Enter a name for the macro, and specify a shortcut key, such as Shift + D (the Ctrl key is automatically added)

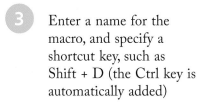

4 Select Personal Macro Workbook (the preferred location for storing macros), add a description, if desired, and then click OK, to start the recording

5 Perform the actions that you want to record, then select the Developer tab, Code group, and click Stop Recording

To check out the macro:

6 Click in a different cell, C5 for example, and press Shift + Ctrl + D to try out the macro

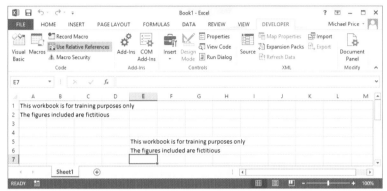

Don't forget

If there are problems with the macro, you may be able to use the Visual Basic Editor to make the changes that are needed (see page 148).

7 The text is entered into the worksheet, in the active cell

The start location changes, because the macro was created with relative references. However, if you click in any specific cells while the macro is being recorded, those references will be honored.

When you have finished checking the macro, close the workbook:

1 Click the File tab, and select Close

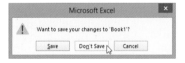

2 Select No, when asked if you want to save changes

Beware

The relative reference applies to the macro, as the initial cell was selected before macro recording was started.

The macro itself will be retained in the Personal Macro Workbook. This will be saved at the end of the Excel session (see page 144).

Active Workbooks Macros
If you selected to store the recorded macro in the active workbook, you must save that workbook as file type .xlsm. You will also need to reset the level of macro security (see page 140).

When you close the active workbook, the macros it contains will no longer be available in that Excel session.

Apply the Macro

1 Open a workbook that requires the disclaimer text, and select the location (e.g. My Personal Budget, cell A16)

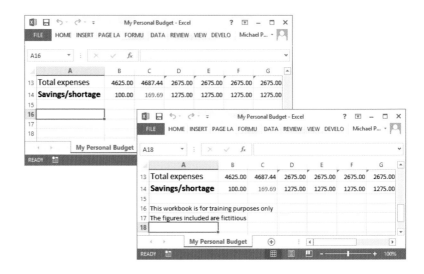

2 Press the shortcut key, Shift + Ctrl + D, to run the macro

3 Save the worksheet (no need to change the file type)

 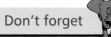
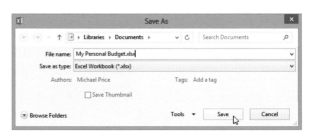

4 When you end the Excel session, you can save your Personal Macro Workbook, and, with it, any macros that you have created during the session

View the Macro

1 Select the View tab, then, from the Window group, click Unhide

2 Select Personal.xlsb, which is your Personal Macro Workbook, and then click OK

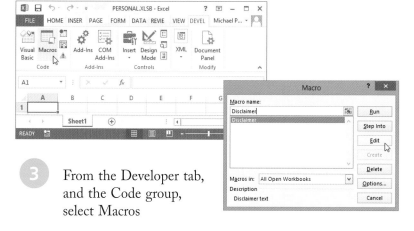

3 From the Developer tab, and the Code group, select Macros

4 Select the macro you want to review and click Edit, to display the code in the VB Editor

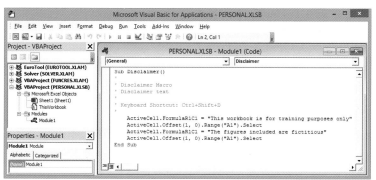

5 Select File and then Save Personal. xlsb, to save any changes. To finish, select File and then Close and Return to Microsoft Excel

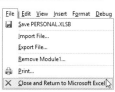

145

Don't forget

You can view and edit the macro. However, since it is stored in a hidden workbook, you must start by making the workbook visible.

Hot tip

You can make changes to the macro, e.g. revise the text that is entered into the cells, even if you don't know the VBA language.

Beware

When you've finished viewing or changing your macros, you should select View, Hide, to hide the Personal Macro Workbook.

Macro to Make a Table

1 Open a share history file, YHOO.csv for example

2 Select Developer, Use Relative References, and then click Record Macro

3 Specify the macro name, shortcut, and description, then click OK, to start recording

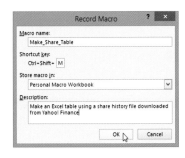

The steps in the process are as follows:

1 Go to cell A3 (the start of the data range):
   Alt H FD G A3 Enter

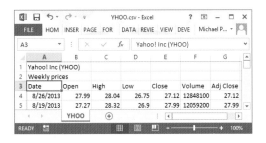

2 Select the whole data range (A3:G910 in this example) using the End and Arrows keys:
   ShiftDown
   End RightArrow
   End DownArrow
   ShiftUp

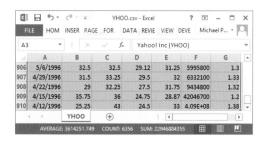

Don't forget

This shows the data range selected, ready for creating the Excel table.

3 Create an Excel Table from the selected set of data:
Alt N T Enter

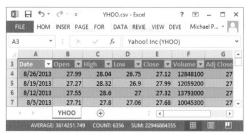

Don't forget

The table is created, but the date column is in descending order (unsuitable for a lookup table).

4 Go to cell A4 (the date field in first row of actual data):
Alt H FD G A4 Enter

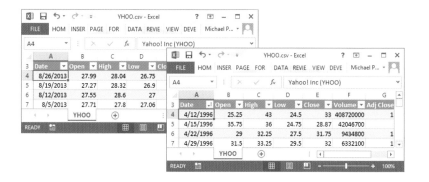

Beware

If you create an Excel table in a .csv file, you must Save As Excel Workbook (.xlsx format), to retain the table (see page 149).

5 Sort the column in ascending date sequence:
Alt A SA

6 Click Developer, Stop Recording, to complete the macro

Edit the Macro

1 Unhide the Personal Macro Workbook (see page 145)

2 Select Developer, and then Macros, from the Code group

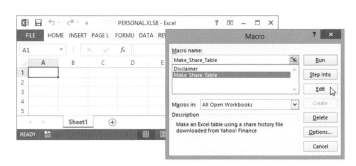

3 Select the Make_Share_Table macro, and click Edit, to display the code in the Visual Basic Editor

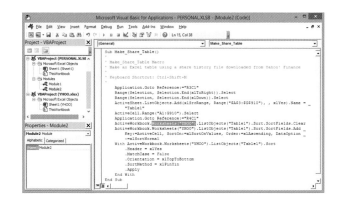

4 Select Edit, Replace, to replace Worksheets("YHOO") by ActiveSheet, and then click the Replace All button

5 To save changes, select File, Save Personal.xlsb (or press Ctrl + S)

6 Select File, Close and Return to Microsoft Excel (or press Alt + Q)

Use the Macro

1 Open another share history file (ibm.csv, for example) that needs to be changed to an Excel table

Beware

As written, the macro assumes that the worksheet will have data in rows 4 to 910 (1996-2013). If there are fewer actual rows, the remainder will appear as empty table rows. Extra rows will be stored after the table.

2 Press the macro shortcut key, Shift + Ctrl + M, and the data range is immediately converted to Excel table format

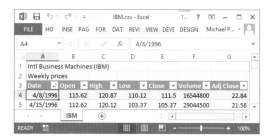

Hot tip

Since the macro now refers to the ActiveSheet, it converts the data range in the current worksheet, without regard to its name.

3 Save the worksheet as file type Excel Workbook (.xlsx)

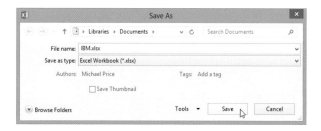

Don't forget

The macro remains in the Personal Macro Workbook, so the share workbooks do not need to be macro-enabled.

Repeat this for any other share history files, which can each be converted to Excel table format with a single click of the Make_Share_Table macro shortcut key.

Follow a similar procedure to create and test macros for any other tasks that you need to complete on a regular basis.

Create Macros with VBA

Hot tip

The Music List from Chapter 3 is used here, to illustrate the use of Visual Basic to create a macro, in this case, to insert page breaks after each album.

① Display the Developer tab on the Ribbon (see page 141)

② Select the Developer tab, and then select Visual Basic

③ Click the VBAProject for Personal.xlsb, and then select Insert, Module

④ In the code window for the module, type (or paste) the code for your macro

Don't forget

This macro identifies the last non-blank row in the worksheet. It checks the values in column 4 (Album name), and inserts a page break whenever the name changes.

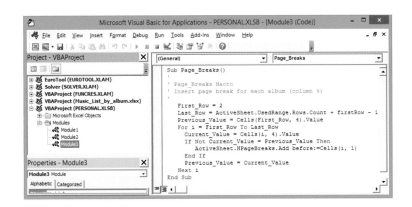

⑤ When you have entered and checked the macro code, select File, Close and Return to Microsoft Excel

You can search on the Internet for example Visual Basic macros, e.g. at **code.msdn.microsoft.com**

6 In the Music_list worksheet, click the Page Break Preview button on the status bar, to see the page setup

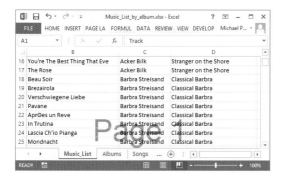

To apply page breaks based on albums:

1 Select the Developer tab, and click the Macros button

2 Select the Page_Breaks macro, and click Run

3 Manual page breaks are inserted at every change of album in the worksheet data range

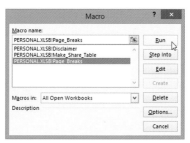

4 Select Page Layout, Print Titles, to replicate the headings on every page

Add Macros to the Toolbar

If you specified a Ctrl or Shift + Ctrl shortcut when you created your macro, you can run the macro by pressing the appropriate key combination. You can also run the macro by clicking the Macros button, from the View tab or the Developer tab. To make macros more accessible, you can add the View Macros option to the Quick Access Toolbar.

1 Select File, Options, and select Quick Access Toolbar, then Choose commands from Popular Commands

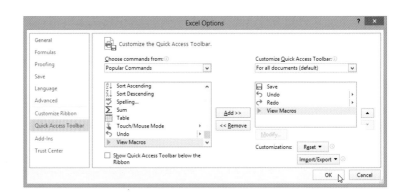

2 Click View Macros, click Add, and click OK, View Macros appears on the Quick Access Toolbar

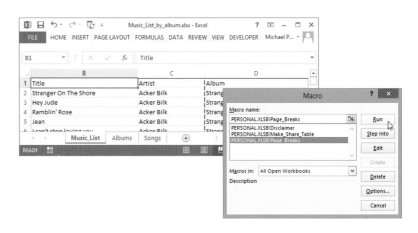

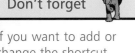
3 To run a macro, click the View Macros button on the toolbar, select the macro that you want, and click Run

Alternatively, you can add macros as individual icons on the Quick Access Toolbar.

1   Open Excel Options, select Quick Access Toolbar, and Choose commands, from Macros

2   Scroll down to the particular macros, select each one in turn, and click Add

3   Each macro will have the same icon. You can click Modify, and select a different icon

4   The icons for the macros are added to the Quick Access toolbar

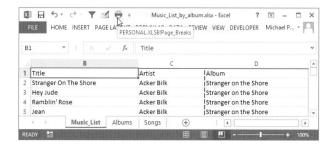

5   The tooltip shows the name of the macro, which runs immediately when you select its icon

Hot tip

Macros can also be associated with graphics, or hot spots on the worksheet.

Debug Macros

If you are having a problem with a macro, or if you are just curious to see how it works, you can run it one step at a time.

1 Select Macros, from Developer (or from View), choose the macro you want to run, and click Step Into

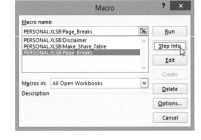

2 Press F8 repeatedly to run through the code, one step at a time

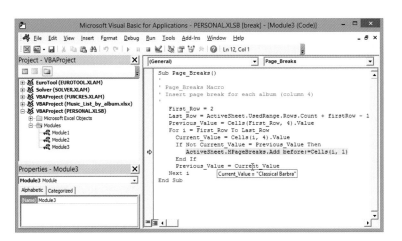

3 Hold the mouse over a variable, to see its current value

4 Select Debug, to see the other testing options available, such as setting breakpoints

5 Press F5 to continue to the next breakpoint (or to complete the macro, if no breakpoints are set)

6 To finish, select File, Close and Return to Microsoft Excel

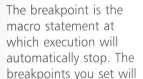

Hot tip

The breakpoint is the macro statement at which execution will automatically stop. The breakpoints you set will not be saved with the code when you exit.

10 Templates and Scenarios

For the most frequent uses of Excel, you'll find ready-made templates to give you a head start. There are more Excel resources at Microsoft Office and other websites. Excel also has special problem-solving tools.

Templates

You can save effort, and you may discover new aspects of Excel, if you base your new workbooks on available templates.

1 Click the File tab, and then click New (or press Ctrl + N), to see the blank workbook and other available templates

2 Review the example templates, or select a category such as Loan to see more templates

Don't forget

The template will be downloaded and a workbook will be opened ready for use, though you can make any changes you wish, if it doesn't exactly meet your requirements.

3 Select the template you want to use, Loan amortization schedule for example, and click Create

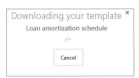
Downloading your template ×
Loan amortization schedule

Cancel

4 The input boxes are predefined with data, so that you can check out the way the workbook operates

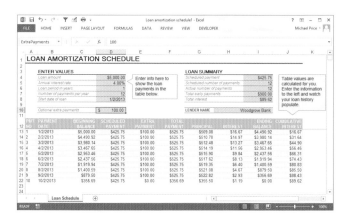

5 Adjust the values, and the worksheet is extended by the number of payments, and displays the calculated amounts

6 To view the formulas behind the calculations, press Ctrl + ` (or select the Formulas tab and click Show Formulas)

7 Select the Formulas tab and click the Name Manager button (or press Ctrl + F3), to see the names defined in the workbook, with values and references

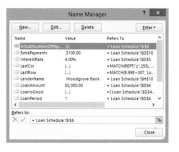

Online Templates

To help in creating a workbook for a particular purpose:

1 Select File, New, click Search for online templates, enter a search term, e.g. exercise, and click the magnifier

Don't forget

The last template that you downloaded and used will be listed in the featured templates ready for possible re-use.

2 Matching templates will be listed, and a series of related subcategories offered, to help focus on the topic

3 Scroll down and you will see that related templates from your other Office applications are also detected

Hot tip

The spreadsheet may be in compatibility mode, since it was originally designed for a previous version of Excel.

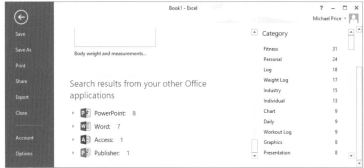

Choose a template to Create and Save a workbook (see page 156)

You can amend the template and save the revised copy in your Documents library for later use:

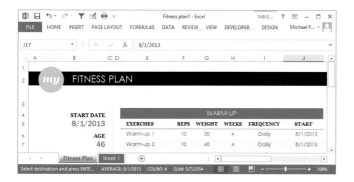

1 Select File, Save As, select My Documents and choose Save as type Excel Template (*.xltx)

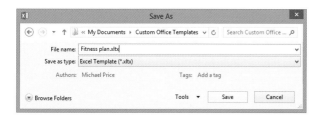

2 The template will be saved in Custom Office Templates in the Documents library

3 Select File, Options, New, Personal to view your templates

More Excel Resources

The Internet is a prolific source of advice and guidance for Excel users at all levels. Here are some websites that may prove useful:

1 Go to **office.microsoft.com** and click Products then scroll down and select Excel from the Office applications

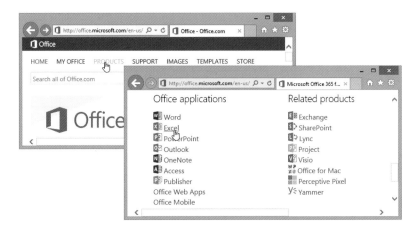

2 Scroll down for links to templates, tutorials and tips for using Excel, and to ask any Excel questions you may have

3 Scroll back up and select the Support option for help getting started, in particular links to Community forums

4 Microsoft MVPs (most valued professionals can provide lots of useful information. Go to **mvp.microsoft.com**

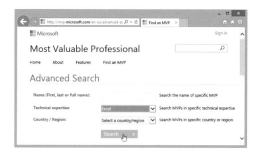

5 Select Find an MVP, click Advanced Search, enter the Technical expertise as Excel, for a list of specialists

If you are interested in creating Excel functions and macros, you should visit the Office and Excel developers' centers

6 Go to **msdn.microsoft.com/office** and select the Excel site

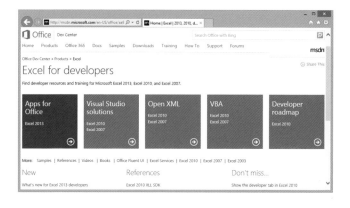

Don't forget

The Developer centers offer information to help you plan, code, build, deploy and migrate solutions for Excel and other Office applications.

Hot tip

You'll find that many references relate to Excel 2010, 2007 or other versions. These will often be just as applicable when you are running Excel 2013.

What-If Analysis

What-If analysis involves the process of changing values in cells, to see how those changes affect the outcome on the worksheet. A set of values that represent a particular outcome is known as a scenario. To create a scenario:

1 Open the worksheet, and enter details for a loan, a 25-year mortgage for example

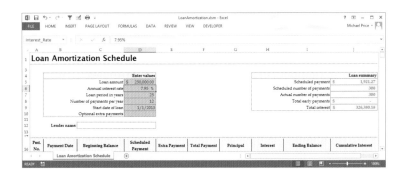

2 Select the Data tab, and, from the Data Tools group, click What-If Analysis, Scenario Manager

3 Click Add, type a scenario name (e.g. X000), enter the address references for the cells that you may want to change, and then click OK

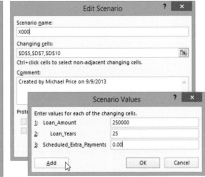

4 Change cells from their initial values, as required, in this case adjusting the value of Scheduled_Extra_Payments

5 Repeat steps 3 & 4 for each scenario, clicking Add then OK, incrementing each by 50 (i.e. X050... X350 and 50.00...350.00), finally clicking OK after the last scenario

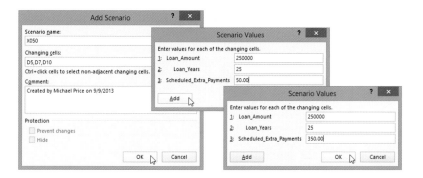

Hot tip

Additional input cells (Loan_Amount and Loan_Years) have been selected. They have been left unchanged for these scenarios, but give the option for other scenarios in a future analysis.

6 Select one of the scenarios, X200 for example, and click Show to display the associated results on the worksheet

7 Select Close, to end the Scenario Manager and return to the worksheet

Don't forget

You can click Edit to make changes, or corrections, to a scenario, or click Delete to remove unwanted scenarios.

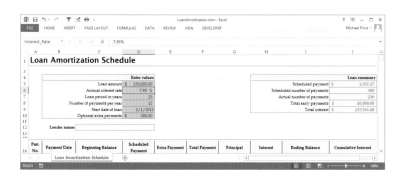

The results from the scenario that was last shown will be displayed. If no scenario was left selected in the Scenario Manager, the original worksheet values will be shown.

Summary Reports

To create a scenario summary report, showing all the possible outcomes on one worksheet:

1 On the Data tab, in the Data Tools group, click What-If Analysis, click Scenario Manager, and then click Summary

2 Choose report type, Scenario summary

3 Enter the references for the cells that you want to track (cells with values modified by the changes in scenario values), in this case J7 (actual number of payments and J9 (total interest)

4 The outcomes for each of the scenarios are calculated, and the results placed on a new worksheet added to the workbook and named Scenario Summary

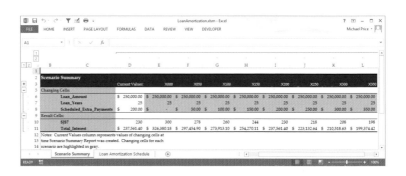

In the Scenario Summary worksheet, the Changing Cells section displays the values for each scenario of the cells that were selected, when the scenarios were created. The Result Cells section shows the values of the cells Payments and Total Interest, specified when the summary report was created. The Current Values column shows the original values, before the scenarios were defined.

...cont'd

The results can also be presented as a Scenario PivotTable report:

1. Open the Scenario Manager, click Summary, choose Scenario PivotTable report, and enter the references for the result cells

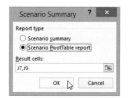

2. The results are shown in a table on a separate worksheet

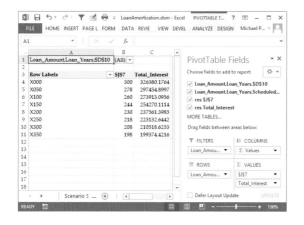

3. Select the PivotTable Tools Analyze tab, then select PivotChart from the Tools group, choose the type of chart, Line Chart for example, and then click OK

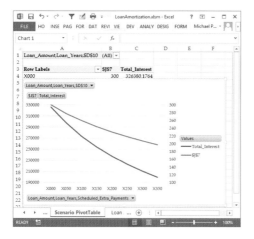

Beware

You must switch back to the Loan Amortization Schedule worksheet, before opening the Scenario Manager.

Hot tip

To generate a Scenario PivotTable report, it is always necessary to specify the relevant result cells.

165

Don't forget

As with any charts, you can select Design, Move Chart, and place the PivotChart on a separate worksheet.

Goal Seek

If you know the result that you want from an analysis, but not the input values the worksheet needs to get that result, you can use the Goal Seek feature. For example, you can use Goal Seek in the Loan Amortization worksheet, to determine the extra payment required to keep total interest below $150,000.

1 Select Data, then What-If Analysis from Data Tools, and then Goal Seek

2 For Set cell, enter the reference for the cell with the target value (cell J9, Total Interest)

3 In the box for the To value, type the result you want (i.e. 150000)

4 In the box for By changing cell, enter the reference for the cell that contains the value you want to adjust (D10, Optional extra payments)

5 The value in D10 is rapidly varied, and the worksheet continually recalculated, until the target value of interest is reached

6 Click OK to return to the worksheet, with the computed results displayed

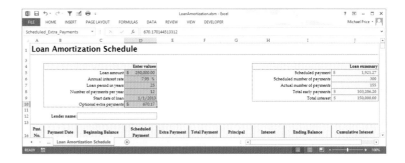

7 Save the results as another scenario, for later reference

Optimization

Goal Seek allows you to solve problems where you want to find the value of a single input, to generate the desired result. It is of no help when you need to find the best values for several inputs. For this, you require an optimizer, a software tool that helps you find the best way to allocate resources. These could be raw materials, machine time, people time, money, or anything that is in limited supply. The best or optimal solution will perhaps be the one that maximizes profit, or minimizes cost, or meets some other requirement. All kinds of situations can be tackled in this way, including allocating finance, scheduling production, blending raw materials, routing goods, and loading transportation.

Excel includes an add-in optimizer, called Solver. You may need to install this (see page 103) if it doesn't appear on your system. To illustrate the use of Solver, we'll examine a product mix problem.

Sample Solver Problem

Imagine that your hobby is textiles, and that you produce craft goods (ponchos, scarves, and gloves). There's a craft fair coming up, and you plan to use your existing inventory of materials (warp, weft, and braid) and your available time (for the loom, and to finish goods). You want to know the mix of products that will maximize profits, given the inventory and time available. These include 800 hanks of warp, 600 hanks of weft, 50 lengths of braid, 300 hours of loom time, and 200 hours of finishing time.

To produce a poncho, you will need 8 units of warp, 7 of weft, 1 of braid, 6 for loom, and 2 for finish. For a scarf, the values are 3 warp, 2 weft, 0 braid, 1 loom, and 1 finish. For a pair of gloves, they are 1 warp, 0 weft, 0 braid, 0 loom, and 4 finish.

You make the assumption that your profit is $25 per poncho, $10 per scarf, and $8 per pair of gloves.

You remember that you need four of each item as samples, to show the visitors to the fair. Also, you recall that usually half the scarves are sold in sets with gloves.

Relationships between the objective, constraints, and decision variables are analyzed to decide the best solution, to satisfy the requirements.

Don't forget

The problem description must be in sufficient detail, to establish the relationships and identify the constraints.

Project Worksheet

The craft fair optimization information (see page 167) can be expressed in a worksheet, as follows:

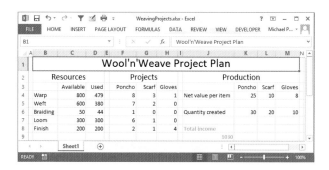

The formulas that are included in the spreadsheet are:

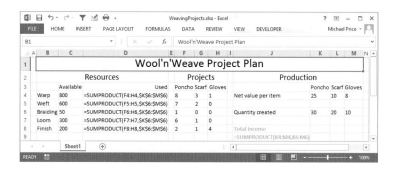

Sample values for the production quantities have been inserted, just to check that the worksheet operates as expected. Excel Solver will be used to compute the optimum quantities.

There are some limitations or constraints that must be taken into account. These are:

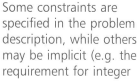

 1 You cannot exceed the available resources

2 There must be at least 4 of each product (samples for the craft show)

3 There must be whole numbers of products (integers)

4 There must be a pair of gloves each, for at least half the scarves (so that sets can be offered for sale)

Solver

To calculate the optimum solution for the craft fair problem:

1 Click the cell J9, which contains the target value Total Income, then select the Data tab, and click Solver in the Analysis group

2 Choose the Max option. Then click the By Changing Cells box, and use the Collapse and Expand buttons to select the product quantities cells (K6:M6)

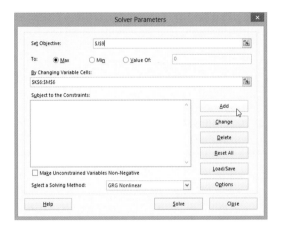

3 Click the Add button, and select cells to specify that resources used must be less than or equal to those available

4 Click Add, and select cells to specify that quantities produced must be greater than or equal to 4

5 Add the constraint that quantities must be integers

169

Hot tip

Solver will use the currently selected cell as the target, unless you replace this reference with another cell.

Don't forget

Click Add, to define the next constraint, or click OK, to return to the Solver Parameters panel.

...cont'd

6 Specify that the quantity of gloves must be at least half the quantity of scarves, and then click OK

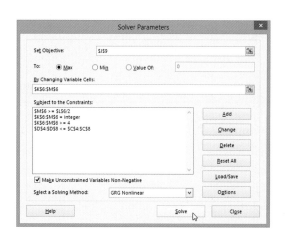

7 Click Solve, and the results are calculated and displayed

8 If Solver finds a solution, click Keep Solver Solution, clear Return to Solver Parameters Dialog, select a report if desired, then click OK, to return to the workbook

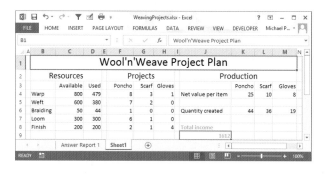

11 Links and Connections

Excel lets you make external references to other workbooks, or to web pages that contain data needed for your active worksheet. Your worksheet is updated automatically, if the source data changes. You can also share your data as an Office document, or as a PDF.

Link to Workbooks

172

Sometimes you may want to refer to the data in one workbook from another, separate workbook. You may, for example, want to provide an alternative view of the data in a worksheet, or to merge data from individual workbooks, to create a summary workbook. You can refer to the contents of cells in another workbook by creating external references (also known as links).

References may be to a cell or a range, though it is usually better to refer to a defined name in the other workbook.

To establish defined names in a source workbook:

1 Open a source workbook, North.xlsx for example

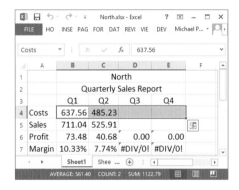

2 Select a range of cells, B4:E4 (the costs) for example

3 Select the Formulas tab, then click Define Name, from the Defined Names group

4 Specify the name (or accept the suggested name, based on the adjacent label, e.g. Costs), and then click OK

5 Repeat the Define Name process for the ranges of Sales (cells B5:E5) and Profit (cells B6:E6)

6 Select the Formulas tab, and click Name Manager, in the Defined Names group, to see all the name definitions

Hot tip

The names will have the same cell references for the associated ranges, as those shown for the North workbook.

7 Save the North workbook to record the ranges names that have been defined

Repeat this for the other source workbooks (in this example, they are South, East, and West), to define the range names Costs, Sales, and Profit in each of them.

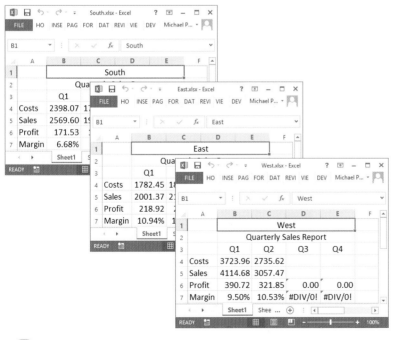

Don't forget

The benefit of links is that, when source workbooks change, you won't have to make changes manually to the destination workbooks that refer to those sources.

173

8 Save and close the South, East, and West workbooks

Create External References

1 Open the source workbooks that contain the cells you want to refer to (e.g. North, South, East, and West)

2 Open the workbook that will contain the external references (in the example, it is called Overall.xlsx)

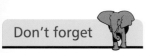

Don't forget

You can incorporate the external reference into a function or formula, as you might with any cell reference.

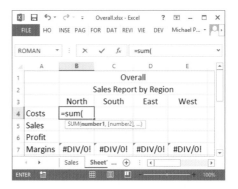

3 Select the cell in which you want to create the first of the external references (e.g. B4) and type (for example) =sum(

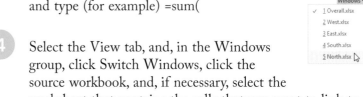

4 Select the View tab, and, in the Windows group, click Switch Windows, click the source workbook, and, if necessary, select the worksheet that contains the cells that you want to link to

5 Press F3, and select the defined name for the range of cells, e.g. Costs, click OK, and then press Enter

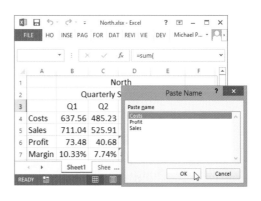

6 Similarly, enter a formula in B5 to sum Sales, and enter a formula in B6 to sum Profit

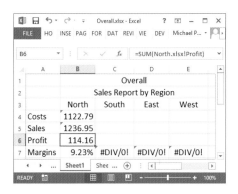

You could refer to source workbook cells directly:

1 Click in cell B8, and type =count(

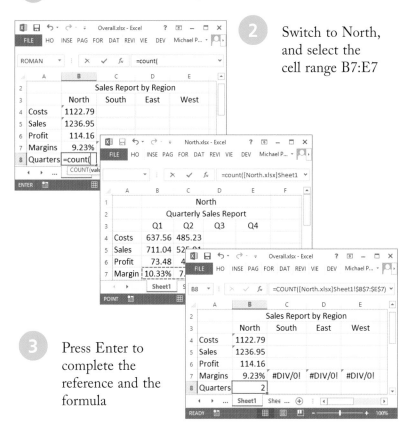

2 Switch to North, and select the cell range B7:E7

3 Press Enter to complete the reference and the formula

Styles of Reference

Don't forget

Quotation marks will be applied to the workbook name, if it contains any spaces, e.g. 'Sales North.xlsx'!Costs

While the source workbooks are open, the links to defined names take the form:

North.xlsx!Costs

Where you refer to cells directly, the links take the form:

[North.xlsx]Sheet1!$B$7:$E$7

Note that the cell references could be relative or mixed, as well as absolute, as shown.

Close the source workbook, and you'll find that the external references are immediately expanded, to include a fully qualified link to the source workbook file.

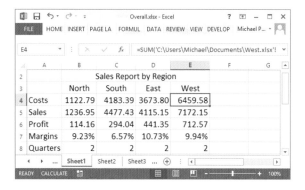

Links with direct cell references also show the file path and name:

Hot tip

The references for South, East, and West have been incorporated. You can do this by selection, as with North, or you can just copy the formulas for North, and change the name appropriately.

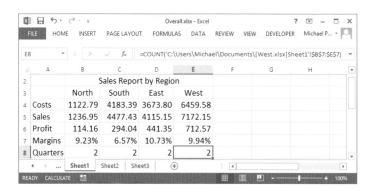

In each case, the path and file name will be enclosed in quotation marks, whether there are spaces included or not.

Source Workbook Changes

Assume that you receive new versions of the source workbooks (with the next quarter's data). You can control how and when these changes affect the destination workbook.

1 Open the destination workbook

2 By default you'll receive a warning message saying there are external links, and offering an option to apply updates

3 Select Don't Update, and the workbook opens, unchanged

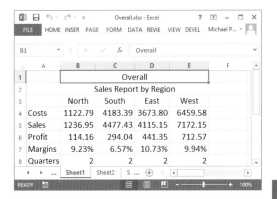

4 Select File, Options, click Advanced and review the settings for external links

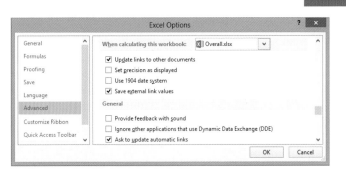

Don't forget

Leave source workbooks closed. When source and destination workbooks are open on the same computer, links will be updated automatically.

Hot tip

Select Update, and the source workbooks will be accessed and any changes will be applied and available when the destination workbook completes opening.

Beware

Do not use this option to turn off the prompt, or you will not be aware when workbooks get updated. Use the workbook-specific option (see page 179) instead.

Apply the Updates

1 Select the Data tab, then, in the Connections group, choose Edit Links

2 Select the links to refresh, and click Update Values

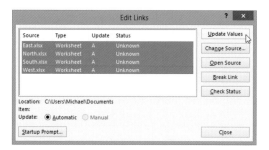

3 Data changes are applied, and worksheet status is updated

4 The updated information is added to the destination workbook, which now displays the data for three quarters

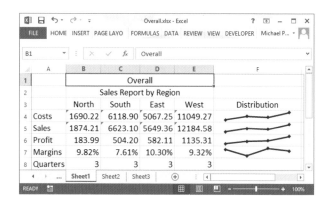

Turn Off the Prompt

If you are confident with the integrity of the external links, you can turn off the update prompt for a specific workbook.

1 Open the workbook and select Edit Links from the Connections group on the Data tab

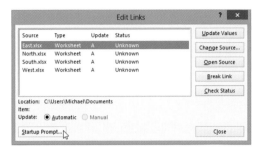

2 Click the Startup Prompt button and choose Don't display the alert and update links then click OK

3 Whenever you open that workbook in future, Excel will automatically check for updates and apply the latest values from the source workbooks

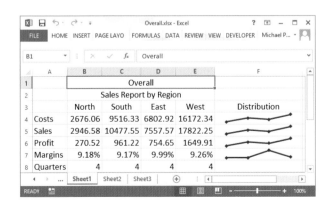

Don't forget

If you choose Don't display the alert and don't update automatic links, users of the workbook won't be aware when the data in the workbook becomes out of date.

179

Save Workbook Online

You can store workbooks and other documents online, and access them via Office Web Apps, or share them with other users. To copy a workbook to the SkyDrive from within Excel:

1 Open the workbook, click the File tab, and select Save As

2 Select the SkyDrive for the current user and click Browse to explore the SkyDrive contents

3 Select the SkyDrive folder, e.g. Project, and click Open

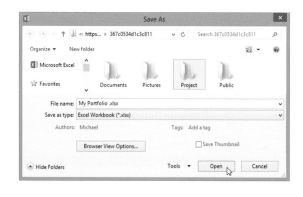

4 Amend the workbook name if required and click Save

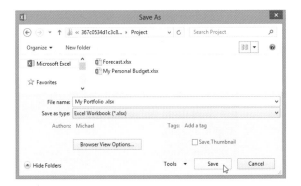

With the workbook on your SkyDrive, you can now access it even on computers that do not have a copy of Excel 2013 installed.

1 Go to **office.microsoft.com** and select My Office

2 Enter the email address that is your Microsoft account

3 Click the SkyDrive link to see all the folders and documents

Hot tip

Once you have saved the workbook to your SkyDrive, you should close it from within Excel if you are planning to open it from within your browser (see page 182).

181

NEW!

Don't forget

At the My Office website you can work with documents from Word, Excel, Powerpoint and OneNote, whether or not you have Office 2013 on your computer.

Using Excel Web App

1 Open your SkyDrive and click the folder that contains the workbook you want to view

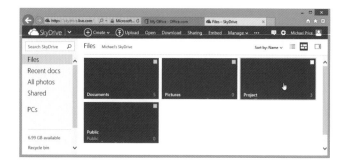

2 When the folder opens, right-click the workbook and select Open in Excel Web App

3 The workbook opens in your browser, for review and with commands for Edit, Share, Data and Find

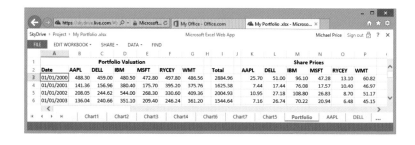

4 Select Edit Workbook and Edit in Excel Web App to open with an abbreviated Excel Ribbon

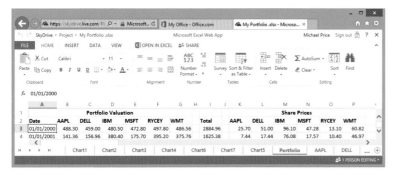

5 Select Open in Excel (or select Edit in Excel from the Edit Workbook command) and the full Ribbon app

6 On a computer without full Excel 2013 you can Edit in Excel Web App, but Edit in Excel gives an error message

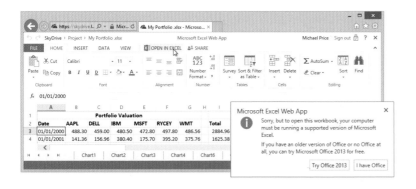

Excel in Word

Hot tip

To share data with others who don't have access to Excel or the Office Web Apps, you can present the information in a Microsoft Office Word document (as illustrated here), or in a PowerPoint presentation.

To add data from an Excel worksheet to your Word document:

1 In Excel, select the worksheet data, and press Ctrl + C (or select Home and click Copy, from the Clipboard group)

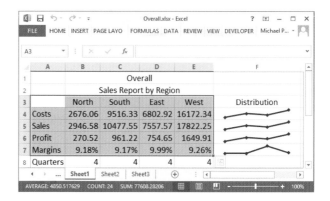

2 Click in the Word document, and press Ctrl + V (or select Home and click Paste, from the Clipboard group)

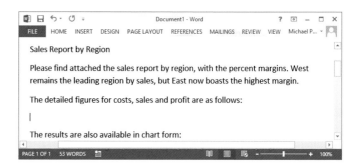

Don't forget

You can paste the data as a table, retaining the original formatting, or using styles from the Word document, as shown. Alternatively, paste the data as a picture or tab-separated text. There are also options to maintain a link with the original worksheet.

3 Click Paste Options, and select the type of paste you want

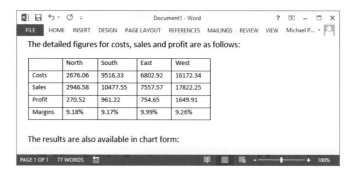

To copy an Excel chart to your Word document:

1 In Excel, select the chart on the worksheet or chart sheet, and press Ctrl + C (or select Home, Clipboard, Copy)

2 In the Word document, click where you want the chart, and press Ctrl + V (or select Home, Clipboard, Paste)

3 Click Paste Options, and select the type you want

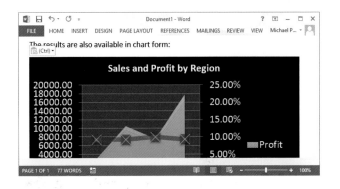

Publish as PDF (or XPS)

To send data to others who do not have Excel or Word, you can publish the workbook in Adobe Acrobat PDF format, which only needs Microsoft Reader in Windows 8 or Adobe Reader in prior versions of Windows.

Hot tip

You can also save as XPS, and the documents can then be viewed using Microsoft Reader in Windows 8 or the XPS viewer in previous versions.

1 Open the workbook in Excel, click the File tab, and then click Save As

2 Set the Save As type to PDF (or XPS)

Don't forget

You can publish the entire workbook, the active worksheet, or selected ranges of cells, as PDF or XPS documents.

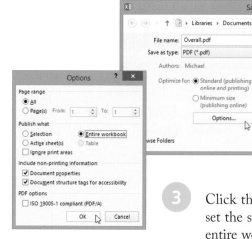

3 Click the Options button, to set the scope, e.g. active sheet or entire workbook, and click OK

4 Select Open file after publishing, and click the Save button, to create and display the PDF (or XPS) file

Hot tip

If you save your workbooks as PDF (or XPS) files, you can be sure that the files you share retain exactly the data and format you intended.

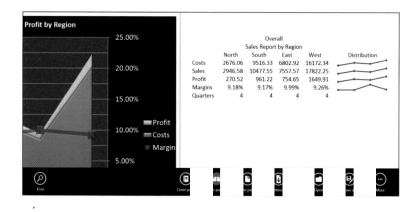

	North	South	East	West
Costs	2676.06	9516.33	6802.92	16172.34
Sales	2946.58	10477.55	7557.57	17822.25
Profit	270.52	961.22	754.65	1649.91
Margins	9.18%	9.17%	9.99%	9.26%
Quarters	4	4	4	4

Index

N

O

P

U

X

V

Y

Z

W